The Meaning of Courtly Love

Papers of the first annual conference
of the
Center for Medieval and Early Renaissance Studies
State University of New York at Binghamton
March 17-18, 1967

Edited by F. X. NEWMAN

STATE UNIVERSITY OF NEW YORK PRESS
ALBANY

Contents

Preface

This book consists of five papers read at a conference sponsored by the Center for Medieval and Early Renaissance Studies of the State University of New York at Binghamton on March 17-18, 1967. A partial transcript of the round-table discussion which concluded the conference follows the texts of the papers. A selected bibliography of recent writings on the subject of courtly love has been appended to the conference record, both to suggest the background of scholarship against which the conference took place and to provide the interested reader with a guide to further exploration of the question.

The papers were originally written to be heard rather than read and, although each speaker has had the opportunity to revise his contribution, none has chosen to make substantial alterations in his original text. These pages are therefore intended to be a written record of what was an oral event and retain, it is hoped, some of the informality and spontaneity that marked the conference itself. The papers, it should be added, are entirely independent of each other. Since the circumstances of the occasion prevented an exchange of texts, the speakers knew only the titles of the other contributions in advance of the conference. Therefore, whatever consistency or conflict the reader may notice as he proceeds from essay to essay is not the product of design, but the result of the commonly felt pressures of the subject itself.

That subject is courtly love (or *amour courtois*, or *höfische Minne*, or *amore corteze*) and the aim of the Center in sponsoring the conference was to prompt a public examination of the vitality of the conception among contemporary medievalists. Ever since

Gaston Paris introduced the term in a famous article in *Romania* in 1883, *amour courtois* has been a conventional part of the critical vocabulary of medieval studies. From the first it was a notion that provoked clashing opinions, some of which are chronicled in Mr. Silverstein's essay. But in recent years the discussion has taken a rather new turn. The central issue in the disputes over *amour courtois* has usually been the problem of its origin. Claims for a variety of sources and influences—Ovid, Catharism, Mozarabic lyricism, Bernardine mysticism, the Provençal sun, and so forth—have been proposed and controverted. Despite their differences, however, scholars seemed able to use the term *amour courtois* with a certain confidence in its mutual meaningfulness. It is easy to show that some of this confidence was misplaced; nonetheless it is true that there has been from the beginning a kind of orthodoxy on the subject, a core of common assumptions. The novelty of much of the recent discussion of courtly love is that it questions, not simply one or another theory of origin, but the content of the term itself. Not long ago, for example, an eminent medievalist published a stock-taking essay on the subject and entitled it "The Myth of Courtly Love." The flat skepticism of that title reflects something of the new tone that has entered the discussion.

Since stock-taking was also the motive for the convening of the present conference, it may be worthwhile to preface the papers themselves with a statement of what it is that is being taken stock of. The simplest and yet the soundest way to do so is to go back to the seminal essay of Gaston Paris. He not only invented the phrase *amour courtois*, but also gave it its original definition. And, to a degree unusual in literary scholarship, his formulation of the question has remained normative.

The immediate subject of Paris's *Romania* essay was Chrétien de Troyes's *Conte de la charrette;* when he proposed the term *amour courtois* he meant it to characterize the love of Lancelot and Guenevere. That love, according to Paris, was of a particular kind: illicit (and therefore furtive), yet marked by an almost religious devotion of the lover to his lady. In a relationship that was "a kind of idolatry," the lover accepts the total superiority of his mistress and humbly attempts to render himself worthy of her by performing whatever daring or ignominious feats she may command. If that were all Paris had to say he would simply have been stating the plain facts of the plot of Chrétien's romance. But he was interested in more than the explication of a single poem. In his view the *Conte de la charrette* was the first and fullest representative of a novel conception of love that had entered medieval French literature and life. The unqualified noun *amour* would not do to characterize so new and striking a phenomenon. *Courtly* love was more than mere passion; it was an art, in the medieval sense of a mental and moral discipline. One could even speak of this kind of love as a "code," implying both a system of rules for conduct and a quasi-judicial method of settling contested points. Though the aim of courtly love was the moral improvement, even the ennobling, of the lover, it was not to be confused with "Platonic" love because it was frankly grounded in sexual passion. (It was, of course, also different from Platonic love—without the quotation marks—since it was heterosexual.)

What is striking about the courtly love which Paris described is how clearly incompatible it was with conventional medieval views on the psychology and theology of sexuality. It was the habit of the men of the Middle Ages to think man the superior of woman, to see sexual union (actual or desired) as permissible only within marriage, to consider sensuality a hindrance to union with the divine. Courtly love involves the contradiction of such views. It is the special mark of *amour courtois* that it entails the simultaneous acceptance of contradictory notions, contradictory at least by the conventional standards of the Middle Ages. That is to say that courtly love is a doctrine of paradoxes, a love at once illicit and morally elevating, passionate and disciplined, humiliating and exalting, human and transcendent. Perhaps the ultimate paradox of courtly love is that a doctrine in many ways so unmedieval should be considered the unique contribution of the Middle Ages to the lore of love.

Paris followed his definition of courtly love with a theory of its origins. He stressed three influences: Ovid, the social conditions of the twelfth-century courts, and the new Provençal poetry. The *Ars Amatoria* of Ovid was widely read but seriously misunderstood by literal-minded medieval readers, who mistook the poet's frivolous pseudo-maxims for sober counsel and believed that he had expounded a system, even a science, of love. This "code" found a ready audience in the twelfth-century French aristocracy, newly taught by English example to appreciate the pleasures of a leisured and polite courtly society. Add to this conjunction the fresh current of intellectualized love lyrics welling up from the Midi—lyrics which taught how refined and elevated the language of love could be—and the emergence of courtly love is explicable. Paris located the convergence of these influences at the court of Champagne during the reign of the Countess Marie, the daughter of Eleanor of Aquitaine. Inheriting her mother's love of the world and its pleasures, as well as her literary tastes, Marie became the catalyst for the emergence of a new literature and sensibility of love. Her court poet Chrétien gave expression to *amour courtois* in verse while her chaplain Andreas codified it in the dry, juridical language of his *De arte honeste amandi*. In the pages of Andreas Capellanus we can see the new social style of the twelfth-century court, a brilliant scene populated by anxious suitors, wandering poets, and gracious ladies. One of the favorite entertainments of the court must have been those quasi-judicial assemblages at which highborn ladies settled subtle *questions galantes* in accordance with the strictures of the code of love. And from Champagne and centers like it the poetry and practice of courtly love spread over Europe; it is with us still.

Such, in outline, is the classic formulation of courtly love. The essays that follow represent a variety of responses to that traditional thesis. Some of the opinions expressed are in rather direct conflict: Mr. Silverstein devotes his paper to the uses of the term courtly love while Mr. Robertson's subject is its uselessness; Mr. Benton and Mr. Singleton differ on the availability of evidence for the reality of courtly love as a fact of social history, and so on. But the more durable impression that the papers as a group convey (and that the less formal interchanges during the conference conveyed) is of an underlying similarity of outlook. That outlook may be characterized, perhaps oversimply, as an uneasiness with the paradoxes that constitute the Paris conception of *amour courtois*. Mr. Robertson, for example, rejects the paradoxical "religion of courtly love" in favor of "idolatrous passion" as the appropriate term for the behavior of a lover who kneels worshipfully before his mistress. In other words, where Paris found paradox Robertson finds irony (the exploitation rather the acceptance of contradiction), and he therefore dismisses the conventional conception of courtly love as "inherently absurd." Mr. Benton's conclusion, arrived at by a different route, is equally radical. He subjects the assumption that courtly love was a part of medieval social history to the test of the archive and finds it wanting. Since in his judgment the notion of courtly love is of no use to historians, he returns it to the literary scholars, but with the obvious implication that it will do them no good either.

The succeeding papers are not nearly so pessimistic about the utility of the term, but neither do they allow it the scope it has had. Mr. Singleton finds the concept of courtly love of real use in marking out the stages of Dante's poetic progress. Yet the central term in his analysis is *play:* the "cult" of courtly love was something apart from, "to one side of," the serious business of life. The medieval philosophical notion of the "double truth" has often been employed in the scholarship on courtly love to explain how the lover could worship both his *midons* and his Lord, and perhaps Mr. Singleton's invocation of play should be seen as a version of this argument. Play, however, as Huizinga pointed out, presumes a limited field of action and, though it may be pursued with great seriousness, it is essentially fictive, "to one side of" life. To speak of courtly love as a game played apart from, rather than in opposition to, Christian belief is to reject the paradoxical tension between the illicit and the ennobling that Paris made the central feature of *amour courtois*.

A similar limitation on the scope of the term is evident in Mr. Jackson's paper. In his view the identifying mark of courtly love in the transactions between the poets of France and Germany was *Minnedienst*, which always implied society as audience and field of action. The service of love, bounded by society's artificial values, is wholly different from the mutual, mystical, and asocial "Tristan love" that Mr. Jackson finds finally characteristic of the German reaction to French love poetry. The German poets saw the "code" of love not as a liturgy but as an etiquette and rejected it as such. Mr. Jackson, then, like Mr. Singleton, finds courtly love useful in coming to understand the work of his chosen authors, but in order to do so he must give it a rather more restricted meaning than it has usually had.

The final paper read at the conference, Mr. Silverstein's, is closest in statement of the question to the traditional view. Mr. Silverstein agrees with Paris making the love of Lancelot and Guenevere central and in finding the "moral" of the tale in the "opposition between carnality and spirit." Yet the title of the essay is "The *Uses* of Courtly Love" and in it Mr. Silverstein assigns the place of honor (the anagogic position) in his four-fold scheme of uses to the "Poetic or Esthetic." He prefers to deal with courtly love as a literary motif, a constituent element of autonomous works, rather than reversing the order by seeing literary works as illustrations of a "generalizing and external hypothesis" about medieval culture. Unlike Mr. Robertson or Mr. Benton, he finds a use for courtly love, but it is a modest one. His statement of the issue empties courtly love of the ideological content that from the start has made it so controversial a conception.

No effort to see underlying agreement can obscure the very real differences among the speakers. At one time or another during the conference courtly love was described as an "impediment to the understanding" of texts, a phrase with "no specific content," a "social reality," a "game," a "code," a "literary convention," an "intellectual exercise," a piece of "fictitious" history—the list could easily be lengthened. There is no way of effecting a simple reconciliation of such a collection of disparate opinions. Still, if no overt consensus was reached by the conferees, the final impression that the conference conveyed to its audience was that "courtly love" is, after all, the name of a scholar's hypothesis, not of a medieval institution. That has often been forgotten. The theory which Gaston Paris advanced in order to contextualize the *Conte de la charrette* has sometimes been taken for recorded fact of medieval history. It is well to remember that when we dispute the meaning of "courtly love" we are debating the validity—descriptive and heuristic—of a term medievalists invented for themselves.

F. X. NEWMAN   *July 1, 1968*
Binghamton, N.Y.

x

The Concept of Courtly Love as an Impediment to the Understanding of Medieval Texts

D. W. ROBERTSON, JR.
Princeton University

I have never been convinced that there was any such thing as what is usually called courtly love during the Middle Ages. However, it is obvious that courtly love does exist in modern scholarship and criticism, and that the idea appeals to a great many people today.

Our evidence concerning medieval people as it appears in court records, historical narratives, and other sources reveals them as being severely practical within the limits of their knowledge, and not at all sentimental. But what modern scholars have described as "courtly love," a thing, I might add, that medieval scholars refrain from describing, is not only impractical but downright inconvenient. For example, as a "courtly lover" I should be constrained to love someone else's wife, unless, that is, I happened to live in England, where, some authorities insist, I might on occasion practice the art with my own wife.[1] The non-English situation is not only inconvenient for the lady, but dangerous, since adultery on the part of a wife in medieval society, as in modern Italy, was not taken lightly by law and custom. In fact, during the late Middle Ages in some areas adultery on the part of the husband was not always regarded with much tolerance either. In late fourteenth-century London, for example, a man and woman taken in adultery were required to be shaved, except for two inches of hair around the head, taken to Newgate Prison, and thence paraded publicly through the streets accompanied by minstrels more than half way across the City to be incarcerated in a small prison in the middle of Cornhill called the Tun.[2] However, a further feature of "courtly love" is that it was frequently "pure," so that wife or no wife what one got for his pains, and these were considerable, was little more than anticipatory elation, presumably identical with a feeling described by the troubadours as "joy." Although at least one modern scholar has described this, quite seriously, as "the highest earthly good," I have personally found no medieval counterparts of *Playboy Magazine*, nor indeed any sort of encouragements then of the kind of vicarious joys we seem to pursue with such avidity today. I should imagine pure courtly love especially inconvenient in England, where one might be a "courtly lover" to his wife, although I should not be surprised to find it adduced any day now to explain the merriment of Merry England and the curious lineage of the True Born Englishman.

We are told further that the lady involved should be of much higher station than the lover, that she should be located at a distance, that the lover should tremble in her presence, and that he should obey her slightest wish. He should, moreover, fall sick with love, faint when he sees a lock of the lady's hair, preserve his chastity, and perform great exploits to attract the attention of the lady. All this seems to me a terrible nuisance, and hardly the kind of thing that Henry II or Edward III would get involved in. But that is not all. The lover should also use all the techniques recommended in the *Roman de la rose*. That is, he should spend all his wealth, employ outrageous flattery, engage in blatant hypocrisy about what he wants, and convince the lady that she can accumulate great wealth and a kind of eternal youth by granting her favors. Of course, I realize that various forms of irrational conduct are now carried out with a "holier-than-thou" air, in the name of sophistication; but I doubt that many medieval noblemen could be persuaded to go so far as to become "courtly lovers," even for the sake of a superior social tone and that great ideal frequently attributed to them, and to modern real estate developments, "gracious living."

The advocates of "courtly love" in my audience are probably

eager to point out by this time that I have generalized too hastily. Some will allege that "courtly love" is represented only by the troubadours, some will say that its secrets are revealed only in the pages of Andreas Capellanus, or, perhaps, in the romances of Chrétien de Troyes. Some will say that it is the ancestor of modern romantic love, while others will allege that modern romantic love has nothing to do with it. A few may state that it is a French invention, and that through it France taught the Western World how to appreciate women properly. This diversity of opinion about the nature of "courtly love" is matched by accounts of its origins, which include such things as Pictish matriarchal customs, Manichaean heresies, neo-Platonism, the scarcity of women in Provençal courts, and the Cult of the Blessed Virgin Mary. In spite of this enormous diversity of learned opinion concerning both the nature of courtly love and its origins, the fact remains that almost any medieval literary work that has anything at all to do with love will inevitably be said to show the "conventions of courtly love." Indeed, in most instances, these "conventions," carefully selected to fit the work in question, will be said to "explain" the work. Students will dutifully repeat this explanation, because students may be led to say almost anything, and those among them who grow up to become teachers will almost inevitably repeat it to their students.

At various times in the past I have sought to show that works presumably illustrative of "courtly love" like the *De amore* of Andreas Capellanus, or the *Lancelot* of Chrétien de Troyes, or the *Roman de la rose,* are, in fact, ironic and humorous.[3] The result of this effort has frequently been a reaction to the effect that the works in question may not advocate "courtly love," but at least they satirize it. That is, "courtly love" is like a see-saw: if a man pushes down hard on one end, the other end comes up, and, behold! it is still there. What is being satirized in the works in question is not "courtly love" at all, but idolatrous passion. Idolatrous passion is not a peculiarly medieval phenomenon. It appears in the Old Testament, for example in the stories of Amnon and Holofernes; it is condemned by Lucretius, who recommended visits to prostitutes to get rid of it; and Ovid wrote a whole treatise, the *Remedia amoris,* supplying techniques by means of which one might extricate oneself from its snare. It seems to be a chronic

3

human weakness, although attitudes toward it change with changes in style. It was glossed over with sentiment by the late eighteenth century, glorified with rebellious individualism by the romantics, and thoroughly sentimentalized by the Victorians. Today it seems to be cherished as a manifestation of the deep needs of the personality, and is frequently greeted with what might be called profound psychological piety. In the Middle Ages, however, the classical attitude toward it remained, although it frequently looks "feudal" or "courtly" because it is described in a medieval setting, and it also looks fairly harmless when it is couched in the delicate conventions of the Gothic style. At that time it had overtones of meaning in Christian thought that made it highly significant as a vehicle for philosophical ideas. Christianity was then recognized as a religion of love, rather than as a cult of righteousness, so that aberrations of love were thought to have far-reaching implications in the conduct of everyday affairs. Because of the broad area of associations connected with it in theology and philosophy, idolatrous love was a useful vehicle for the expression of literary and poetic themes. But it was not regarded in terms of sentiment, romantic rebelliousness, sentimentality, or, that great criterion for aesthetic appeal in modern novels, plays, and television programs, stark psychological realism.

Medieval love poetry is extremely varied. There are poems expressing sexual desire, although these are usually not "lyrical" in the modern sense; poems sung in praise of great ladies; crypto-religious poems, written, like the Song of Songs, in terms of physical love; popular songs that do not differ much, except for a certain lack of sentimentality or crypto-sentimentality, from popular songs written today. Aside from the lack of lyrical subjectivity and sentimentality, medieval poetry sometimes shows what might be called frank physical optimism. The medieval troubadour was a Latin, and like some Latins today, he tended to regard women functionally, that is, with an eye to their potentialities either as bed companions or as childbearers. The required qualities are frequently identical. It was possible, moreover, to contemplate and even to celebrate these potentialities in a disinterested way, without feeling any deep personal urge to exploit them. Moreover, the ladies seem to have enjoyed being praised for the physical assets peculiar to their sex. Neither the troubadours nor their successors in the Middle Ages dwell much on sentimental attributes: locks of hair curling over the ear or forehead, little tilts of the nose, characteristic gestures, or other endearing individual traits. The general attitude extends frequently to the Blessed Virgin, and poems addressed to her often display what is to our psychologically sensitive ears a shocking concern for her red lips, white teeth, straight back, graceful shoulders, and so on.[4] But she was, after all, a woman, and, presumably sufficiently beautiful to become the Mother of God.

Although medieval love poetry displays what is to us a certain lack of appreciation for the richness of the human personality, its variety is sufficiently great so that the label "courtly love" is hardly adequate to describe it. Indeed, there are times when the use of this label simply turns the poems upside-down, so that we have little chance of understanding them at all. To illustrate this process, I have chosen two examples from the poetry of Chaucer. Let us begin with an early work, *The Book of the Duchess*.

The standard interpretations of *The Book of the Duchess* all stem from the account of the poem developed many years ago by Professor Kittredge. There have been strong disagreements among scholars about the nature of the malady experienced by the speaker at the beginning of the poem, and about whether the dreamer in the poem is a naïve and inept fool or a skilful guide and counsellor. But almost everyone agrees that the Black Knight is at least in part a representation of John of Gaunt, Duke of Lancaster, and that, whatever else he may be, he is an ideal courtly lover, belonging to the sub-type: English courtly lover of his own wife. Although the portrait of Blanche, if it can be called a portrait, that appears in the poem is highly stylized, we are told that she is made to represent an ideal "courtly mistress." This is a dubious compliment. But, in any event, the poem as a whole is said to illustrate the transference of current French fashions about courtly love to English soil, where they were somehow made appropriate to an elegy for a great lady.

I think it is proper to ask what Professor Kittredge's assumptions about love were when he wrote his interpretation of the poem. This is what he said:

5

Now there is nothing new in the Black Knight's story, either in form or substance. The experience he describes is typical, and he speaks throughout in the settled language of the chivalric system. Love was the only life that became the gently nurtured, and they alone were capable of love. Submission to the god was their natural duty; in his grace and favor was their only hope; for no man's heart was in his own control.[5]

We are led to believe, that is, in rather touching language, that the English nobility subjected themselves to Cupid, and that their "only hope" lay in that god's favors. Medieval views on this subject were quite different. For example, in 1346 the distinguished Mertonian, Thomas Bradwardine, who was at the time Chancellor of St. Paul's and Master of the London schools generally, delivered a sermon celebrating English victories at Crécy and in Scotland. Of the conquered enemies of England, he said in part,

> Embracing a seventh error, they seem to emulate antique pagans worshiping Hymen or Cupid, the god of carnal love. Soldiering in Venus, associating themselves with the retinue of Aphrodite, they think the vigor of their audacity to be probity, victory, or triumph. But they say that no one can be vigorous unless he is amorous, or loves amorously, that no one can fight strenuously to excess unless he loves to excess. But how profane is this foolishness, how false, insane, and wild! . . . They labor strenuously in arms to make for themselves a name like the name of the greatest upon earth. . . . And why do they wish such a name? That they may be loved by foolish women. . . . And who gives them the payment and reward for their labors? Who, except for the god for whom they fight, to whom they devote themselves, and whom they worship? And what payment or reward do they get for their pride? Public and immense disgrace. And for their lechery? A stinking and intense burning.[6]

Bradwardine goes on to explain that devotion to Cupid or Venus is actually enervating, and that English restraint in this matter partially accounts for the victories of English chivalry.

It is obvious that our representatives of Harvard and Merton were not talking about the same thing. To begin with the first, Professor McLuhan has assured us, and I think properly, that most of us look at the world through a rear-view mirror. I might add that this mirror does not give us a very distant view into the past, and, moreover, that it is frequently tilted upward toward the clouds. Both the god of love and the "gently nurtured" as they are alluded to by Professor Kittredge clearly belong to the realm of romantic and Victorian fiction, and have nothing to do with the Middle Ages. He had in mind a sentimental passion only faintly and enticingly tinged with sex, a tinge made decorous by reference to the uncontrolled "heart." Bradwardine, on the other hand, regarded Cupid and Venus as figures for lecherous desire, pure and simple. His insistence, moreover, that lechery or amorous passion is destructive of chivalry is a commonplace of medieval thought from the twelfth century onward among both religious and secular writers on the subject. In so far as Chaucer is concerned, the references to Venus in his work are all consistent with the view expressed by Bradwardine. His two most famous descriptions of her temple, in the Knight's Tale and in *The Parliament of Fowls,* are derived largely from Boccaccio's *Teseida,* and Boccaccio himself informs us in his notes to that work that Venus represents irrational concupiscence.[7] It is hardly surprising that in this temple Palamon vows to make "werre alwey with chastitee," and it would be difficult to describe this vow as being either very noble or very chivalrous.

To return to *The Book of the Duchess,* it should have been clear in the first place that the Black Knight could hardly be regarded as an admirable figure in the poem. He explicitly describes his loss as a loss to Fortune in unmistakably Boethian terms. Anyone who has read *The Consolation of Philosophy* with any care, and not simply as a source for more or less meaningless labels, knows that subjection to Fortune was regarded as a kind of foolishness brought on by too much concern for mere externals. The Black Knight is not only foolish in this respect; he is also very clearly suffering from sloth, a vice regarded during the Middle Ages as stemming from a lack of fortitude. No one in Chaucer's audience would have regarded lack of fortitude and subjection to Fortune as "chivalric" qualities. The fact that advocates of "courtly love" cheerfully embrace them as characteristics of the doctrine they advocate is simply another indication of the inherent absurdity of the doctrine itself. As for John of Gaunt, it may be that the grief he suffered at the death of Blanche in 1369 may have led him temporarily into an attitude somewhat resembling that of the Black Knight, but this does not mean that the Black Knight *is* John of Gaunt. John of Gaunt was a Duke, not a knight. To put this very simply, when the time for paying poll taxes came around, the Duke of Lancaster paid more than any other man in England.[8] Earls paid somewhat less, and mere knights still less. Chaucer did not put a Black Duke in his poem. There are other reasons for not associating the Black Knight too closely with the Duke, but in spite of these facts, preconceived notions of "courtly love" turned the Black Knight into a kind of romantic hero and exemplar of true chivalry. That is, the concept of "courtly love" has prevented generations of scholars from seeing that if the figure of the Black Knight makes any sense at all in the poem, it is intended as a criticism of an attitude toward the deceased Duchess of Lancaster. Those who grieved for her immoderately, like the Black Knight, were thinking of her as mere flesh and blood, an attractive object of desire forever lost. Needless to say, this attitude neglects the lady's more human qualities: her virtues and the value of her memory as an inspiration to chivalric conduct. And it is just these qualities that are celebrated in the poem.

If there was, during the Middle Ages, any such thing as "chivalric love," it was the medieval precedent for the kind of love any Englishman is still supposed to have, however faintly, for his King or Queen. Every subject was expected to love his overlord, man or woman, and his overlord's wife if the overlord happened to be a man. Great ladies like Blanche of Lancaster might have expected the love and devotion of all those in their households, and of many lords, knights, squires, and clerks in other households besides. Blanche of Lancaster specifically was a national figure, the greatest lady in England at the time of her death. But this love was a disinterested devotion, somewhat like that inspired by the Blessed Virgin during the Middle Ages.[9] It had nothing whatsoever to do with either sex or sentimentality, and could not be associated with Cupid or Venus in any way. We have become so preoccupied in recent years with "personality" and the "inner life" that this sort of thing has become very difficult to understand. Nevertheless, this is the kind of love that Chaucer undoubtedly felt and expected others to feel for Blanche. With the love of Sir Lancelot for Guenevere or the love represented as that of the dreamer in the *Roman de la rose*, a poem that ends with a thinly veiled description of sexual intercourse, it has nothing whatsoever in common.

For a second and final example of the kind of obfuscation that results from "explaining" medieval poems in terms of "courtly love" let us turn very briefly to *Troilus and Criseyde*. The protagonist belongs, of course, to another English sub-species of the type: he is a "courtly lover" of a widow. Nevertheless, Professor Robinson assures us, he is an "ideal courtly lover."[10] Like other ghosts, the "ideal courtly lover" takes many forms. As the poem is usually described, its appeal is essentially romantic; it is a tragic and moving story of love in flower and love in frustration. It is consistent perhaps with that eternal pattern of dashed hopes so movingly described by Camus in *The Myth of Sisyphus*, a pattern with which all of us seem to acquire a certain experience. It is not difficult now, in fact, to talk about it in terms of "archetypes," another family of ghosts that clank their chains through modern academic halls. Now it is true that the obvious relevance of *The Consolation of Philosophy* to the thematic development of this poem should have prevented any such concept of it from arising, but "courtly love" is more pleasant to talk about than the philosophical intricacies of Boethius, and it is much easier to talk about it than it is to get students to read *The Consolation*.

Before we consider the poem itself, I think it might be proper to ask ourselves why Chaucer was interested in the story of Troy. The obvious answer, of course, is that the story was popular during the Middle Ages and that Chaucer read Boccaccio's *Filostrato* in some form, liked it, and wrote a poem based on it. But this does not answer our question very specifically. Chaucer probably finished *Troilus* in the latter part of 1386 or in 1387. He was living at the time above Aldgate in London in the apartments granted him by the Mayor and Aldermen of the City in 1374. In this connection, we should remember that the Mayor of London ranked as an Earl, the aldermen as barons or tenants-in-chief of the Crown, and Chaucer as a squire. Although the city of London itself enjoyed increasing prosperity, with some interruptions, during the later fourteenth century, England as a whole did not. There was, in the first place, a severe agricultural depression that created considerable uneasiness among the feudal nobility who were largely dependent upon agricultural production. At the same time, after 1369 the rivalry with France went badly for the English, so that by the end of the century the French court had replaced the English court as the center of European chivalry. The behavior of Edward III in his latter years was, to say the least, unedifying, especially in view of his neglect of the realm and his besotted concern for Alice Perrers, who, incidentally, had a sumptuous residence in London. King Richard was never able to live up to the promise he showed in confronting the rebels in 1381. The nobility was factious, and Parliament reflected their intrigues. The Parliament of 1386 indulged in fanciful accusations against the King's friends, and was probably instrumental in depriving Chaucer of his position at the Custom House. And in 1388 the Merciless Parliament proceeded to more or less wholesale judicial murder. Armed bands roamed the countryside; the court was sapped by intrigue and rumors of intrigue; brawling and disorder broke out not only in the country and in the streets of the towns, but even before the royal justices in the King's Bench. In short, the ties of the old feudal hierarchy seemed to be breaking down in favor of self-seeking, personal ambition, and greed. As Chaucer himself put it, in a poem probably written at Aldgate,

> . . . in oure dayes nis but covetyse,
> Doublenesse, and tresoun, and envye,
> Poyson, manslauhtre, and mordre in sondry wyse.

Under these circumstances it was natural that men should turn to the traditions of the past to find inspiration for reform. Some of Chaucer's friends were "Lollard Knights" who exhibited a remarkably serious concern for traditional Christian moral doctrine.[11] Chaucer's old patron, John of Gaunt, was the patron and devoted friend of the famous reforming mayor of London, John of Northampton.

Where would a Londoner, concerned about decay in the society around him, look for the traditions of his city? In 1419 when Richard Whittington was mayor, the Clerk of the City, John Carpenter, compiled a *repertorium* of city customs based on documents, some of them very ancient, available at the Guildhall. This book became a standard reference, known, because of its original binding, as the *Liber Albus*. Carpenter was a man with whom

Chaucerians should sympathize, for he left a number of books in his will that we know were familiar to Chaucer, including the *De planctu Naturae* and the *Anticlaudianus* of Alanus de Insulis, the *De miseria humanae conditionis* of Innocent III, and the *Philobiblon* of Richard de Bury. Incidentally, the tradition of Richard de Bury's inspiration was quite strong at St. Paul's during the latter fourteenth century. Concerning the City of London the *Liber Albus* tells us,

> In the year from the beginning of the World 4032, and before the Lord's Incarnation 1200, the city that is now called 'London,' founded in imitation of Great Troy, was constructed and built by King Brut, the first monarch of Britain, being at first called 'New Troy,' and afterwards 'Troinovant' . . . .[12]

Another passage, which may be an addition to the text but is said to be based on "ancient books," elaborates this idea:

> Among the noble cities of the world which fame has rendered illustrious, the City of London is the one principal seat of the realm of England which diffuses far and wide the celebrity of its name. It is happy in the salubrity of its climate, in the enjoyment of the Christian religion, in its liberties so well deserved, and its foundation at a most ancient date. Indeed, according to the testimony of the chronicles it is much older than the City of Rome; for, springing from the same more ancient Trojans, London was founded by Brut, in imitation of great Troy, before the foundation of Rome by Remus and Romulus; whence it is that, even to this day, it possesses the liberties, rights, and customs of the ancient city Troy, and enjoys its institutions.[13]

We may remember that the Merciless Parliament accused the then former Mayor of London, Nicholas Brembre, of wanting to change the name of London to "Petty Troy," to declare himself Duke, and to execute several thousands of his opponents. The charge was ridiculous, but the mention of the word *Troy* probably added to its initial plausibility. In any event, the judicial murder of Brembre duly ensued.

Troy, then, served as the great exemplar of the City of London specifically and of the realm of England generally, an idea that we can see operative in *Sir Gawain and the Green Knight*, although it is true that the purport of that work has been obscured by talk about "courtly love." The fall of Troy loomed as a warning to all Englishmen. It came about as a result of the choice made by Paris, who thought Venus, or the life of pleasure and self-satisfaction, more attractive than either Juno, the active life, or Pallas, the life of contemplation or wisdom. The result was the rape of Helen, a lady not venerated in the Middle Ages as she came to be in the pages of Yeats or Camus. The action was an insult to Pallas or wisdom, who had been, so to speak, a kind of patron saint of Troy. To understand the implications of these fabulous events, we should remember that wisdom was regarded throughout the Middle Ages as a royal virtue, proper to kings and princes, and in the individual the supreme control over the passions. Christ was conventionally called *Sapientia Dei Patris*, the Wisdom of God, and the Blessed Virgin was sometimes associated with Pallas, since she had brought Wisdom to mankind. As Raoul de Preslles says in his commentary on *The City of God*, so long as Minerva or *Sapience* ruled the city, Troy was full of virtue, but when she lost her *seignorie*, the city reverted to fleshly lusts and idolatry and thus became doomed to fall.[14]

Boccaccio's poem contained the story of a young prince of Troy who fell passionately in love with a young widow and lost her. His name, "Troilus" in English, suggested a Latin form meaning "Little Troy," so that it was not difficult to make the downfall of Troilus an analogue of the downfall of Troy itself. Just as Venus, or the cultivation of Venus, brought about the destruction of Troy, so also it brought about the destruction of Troilus. The general moral situation is clear enough in Boccaccio, but it had a specific applicability to London and to England as a whole that made it peculiarly suitable for Chaucer's use. Chaucer could refurbish the old object lesson in a new guise, and, with very little difficulty, use Troilus to typify the kind of individual action that brought about the downfall of the City. It does not matter especially whether Chaucer believed the Trojan origin of London literally; the story was well known, and its poetic implications were sufficient. It seems to me that the first step we should make in our understanding of the poem is a recognition of the fact that medieval poetry generally is functional in the society that produces it. It does not have a "reality of its own." Nor was Chaucer a detached historian of past events. The real subject of *Troilus and Criseyde* lies in the life around Chaucer and not in the remote Trojan past. No one in the fourteenth century thought of art as existing "for its own sake." Art was, rather, a vehicle for cherished ideas designed to be practical in its effects.

In the light of these considerations, the general purport of the poem becomes fairly obvious. However, it might be well to point out certain specific features that appear in it to suggest their general significance. In this very hasty account, I shall emphasize what might be called "social" considerations rather than those philosophical aspects of the poem that I have discussed in another place, although it is true that what we call social and political ideas were discussed in moral terms during the Middle Ages. The action of the poem begins at a festival of Pallas in Troy. Since Pallas is the deity of wisdom and what happened to Troy was the result of neglecting her, this scene has considerable thematic importance. Instead of paying any attention to the civic ceremonies, Troilus and his companions are wandering around

> Byholding ay the ladies of the town.

That is, they are tempting Cupid instead of worshiping Pallas. The arrow flies and sends the young Prince of Troy to his chamber alone, where he begins to dream about Criseyde's *figure*. Very soon he is saying to himself

> "myn estat roial I here resigne
> Into hire hond."

We should notice that it is his royal estate, not his person, that Troilus surrenders so quickly to a woman he does not really know. If we remember that there is a sense in which Troy is London, or the realm of England, what we are witnessing is an action typifying the beginning of that decay that Chaucer could see so well in the life around him. To make this idea clear, Chaucer adds that Troilus becomes very fearful, but not fearful concerning the condition of the city. He is afraid of not being able to win Criseyde:

> Alle other dredes weren from him fledde,
> Both of th'assege and his savacioun.

13

He goes out to fight Greeks, not for the "rescous of the town," but to win the kind of Venereal fame Bradwardine thought appropriate to defeated Frenchmen. The opening action of the poem is thus a thematic echo of the Judgment of Paris. Troilus has spurned Pallas and embraced Venus. At the same time, he has abandoned the interests of his community in favor of self-interest and self-satisfaction.

Perhaps I should pause briefly to emphasize the fact that I am not trying to make Chaucer a Puritan. No one expected medieval noblemen to observe strict chastity. But it is one thing to engage in occasional dalliance and quite another to abandon oneself completely to idolatrous passion. Any man in a position of responsibility who devoted himself entirely to any kind of self-interest could hardly be considered admirable. The fact that we are able to romanticize the behavior of Troilus is due to post-Renaissance cultural developments that Chaucer could not possibly have foreseen.

After Pandarus has promised to get Troilus anyone, even his own sister if that is desirable, he leads Troilus in a prayer to Cupid, asking forgiveness for his earlier jokes about love and lovers. He is soon praying also to "blisful Venus" and beseeching Pandarus on his knees to help him. All this "religious" activity has usually been rendered harmless by what has been called "the religion of courtly love." It is, of course, actually a bitter comment on the substitution of "covetyse" and "doublenesse" for the devotion that had made London "happy . . . in the enjoyment of the Christian religion." We see Troilus praying to Venus again in Book II after Pandarus has won a kind of qualified assent from Criseyde and has learned that what she is chiefly concerned with is her "honor," which means for her not the virtue itself, but worldly reputation. Incidentally, the anticipatory "joy" supposed to be characteristic of "courtly love" is here described, just as Bradwardine described it, as a fire. It grows warmer the closer Troilus gets to his goal and is not extinguished after he has attained it. The "doublenesse" apparent in Criseyde's conception of honor is further emphasized in the technique used by Pandarus to bring the lovers together. That is, he lies to both Deiphebus and Criseyde. It is not accidental that the ruse he employs recalls the story of Amnon, whose affair led to civil war.

Medieval men had a strong sense of social hierarchy. Disturbances in society were thought of as violations of that hierarchy, and failures to maintain the integrity demanded by one's estate or degree were thought to be productive of social chaos. Chaucer plays amusingly on this theme in Book III. At the opening, in the house of Deiphebus, Criseyde approaches Troilus as he lies in bed feigning sickness with a request for "lordship" and protection. But what she receives is a promise from Troilus that he will be under her "yerde." The phrase *sub virga*, which this promise reflects, was conventionally used to describe the condition of children, or, occasionally, of wives. Although this inversion is amusing on the surface, the implications for "New Troy" are hardly comic. We can see an analogy to this situation in the punishment for "common brawlers" decreed in the City of London by John of Northampton. A convicted "brawler" was to be led through the City with minstrelsy holding a distaff with tow on it in his hand and placed in the "thews" or stocks designed especially for women, the implication being that his unruliness deprived him of the worth proper to the masculine estate. The predicament of the "brawler" as he holds his distaff is amusing, but the implications of his presence are nevertheless serious. To call Troilus' desire to be under Criseyde's "yard" a manifestation of "courtly love" is a little like saying, quite seriously, that the distaff in the hand of the brawler is a sign of the irrepressible medieval reverence for women.

The theme of the inverted hierarchy is clear enough in Troilus' complete submission to Venus and to Fortune in Book III. It receives an added emphasis on a social level in Book IV, where the Trojan Parliament is shown considering whether to turn Criseyde over to the Greeks in exchange for Antenor. Hector, who is an exemplar of chivalry in the poem, takes a firm attitude:

> "We usen here no wommen for to selle."

But he is overcome by "noyse of peple" as furious as a fire blazing in straw. The image is probably intended to recall the proverbial fire in the bed-straw and to emphasize the analogy between the fury of the people and the passion of Troilus. Chaucer had undoubtedly had plenty of experience with "noyse of peple" in London; and the scene, as others have pointed out, is probably a comment on English Parliaments, perhaps a specific reflection of the Parliament of 1386.[15] The passage looks forward to a similar one in the Clerk's Tale:

> O stormy peple! unsad and evere untrewe!
> Ay indiscreet and chaungynge as a fane!

In neither instance is the poet simply making an historical observation; he is calling attention to something very real in the life of his times. For Chaucer, who had not enjoyed the benefits of the French Revolution, passionate popular outbursts were an inversion of the natural order of sovereignty in the commonwealth. They boded ill for Great Troy and New Troy alike.

The decision of the Trojan Parliament emphasizes the helplessness of Troilus in the situation he has created for himself. He cannot, for shame, reveal his own connection with Criseyde, and he cannot, because of what she calls her "honor," take her away stealthily. He can only blame Fortune, whom he has always honored, he says, "above the goddes alle," and the god of love, who seems to have "repeled" his grace. The two go together, both in the individual and in the state. That is, if the state succumbs to the passions of the people, disregarding its ordered hierarchies in the pursuit of self satisfaction, it is, in effect, worshiping Venus and subjecting itself to Fortune. That is why Chaucer is able to say in Book V,

> Fortune . . .
> Gan pulle awey the fetheres brighte of Troie.

A city or a realm can, like a man, give rein to its passions and subject itself to the whims of Fortune. It can also enjoy what Bradwardine calls the reward of Cupid, "a stinking and intense burning."

When Troilus has found his death on the battlefield, a death deliberately sought in despair and hence a form of suicide, and the city, having lost Hector, is dying also as a result of its own foolishness in abandoning Pallas, the poet adds a stanza that includes a reference to paganism:

> Lo here, of payens corsed olde rites,
> Lo here, what alle hire goddes may availle,
> Lo here, thise wrecched worldes appetites!

The "worldes appetites" and the "goddes" are essentially the same thing. Chaucer is not engaging in idle moralizing; he is condemning exactly the same kind of weakness that Bradwardine attributed to the conquered French in 1346, who "seemed to emulate antique pagans, worshiping Hymen or Cupid, the god of carnal love." Chaucer obviously felt that the English might be doing the same thing, so that New Troy stood in danger of suffering the fate of Great Troy, whose "liberties, rights, and customs" it preserved.

To call Troilus a "courtly lover" caught in the snares of a romantic universe, and to grow sentimental over his fate, is simply to disregard the text of the poem and to foster a kind of historical desecration. From a literary point of view, the "courtly love" interpretation takes all of the humor out of the poem, and, at the same time, substitutes lustful or, if you prefer, "psychological" seriousness for the poem's true serious purpose. We have done the same kind of thing with a great many other medieval works. Even Arcite in the Knight's Tale, who says that "positif lawe" is "broken al day for love," and excuses his own conduct on the ground that a lover simply has to have his beloved whether she is a "mayde, widwe, or elles wyf" has been turned into an ideal "courtly lover" and made a hero. Do my colleagues really believe that Chaucer had no moral or social responsibility? I think it is time we stopped teaching medieval texts to the tune of "Hearts and Flowers." The sophistication of the tune with things like pseudo-Albigensian heresies, pseudo-Platonic philosophies, or pseudo-Arabic doctrines does not conceal its true nature, nor do these wailing ghosts on the sidelines make it any more respectable intellectually. The study of courtly love, if it belongs anywhere, should be conducted only as the subject is an aspect of nineteenth and twentieth century cultural history. The subject has nothing to do with the Middle Ages, and its use as a governing concept can only be an impediment to our understanding of medieval texts.

Notes

1. E.g., see John Lawlor, "The Pattern of Consolation in *The Book of the Duchess,*" *Speculum,* XXXI (1956), 626–48.

2. *Liber Albus,* trans. H. T. Riley (London, 1861), p. 396.

3. E.g., in *A Preface to Chaucer* (Princeton: Princeton University Press, 1962), pp. 195–203, 391–452.

4. See the interesting discussion by James I. Wimsatt, "The Apotheosis of

Blanche in *The Book of the Duchess*," *JEGP*, LXVI (1967), 26–44. A good example is described by Charles Schmidt, "Gottfried de Hagenau," *Revue d'Alsace*, XXIV (1873), esp. pp. 164–65.

5. *Chaucer and His Poetry* (Cambridge, Mass.: Harvard University Press, 1933), p. 63.

6. *Sermo Epinicius*, ed. H. A. Oberman and J. A. Weisheipl, *Arch. d'hist. doct. e. litt. d. m. a.*, XXV (1958), 323–24.

7. Ed. Aurclio Roncaglia (Bari: G. Laterza, 1941), p. 417.

8. R. R. Sharpe, *Calendar of Letter-Books . . . of the City of London: Letter-Book H* (London, 1907), p. 129, note.

9. On this feature of Marian devotion, see Dom Jean Leclercq, *La liturgie et les paradoxes chrétiens* (Paris: Editions du Cerf, 1963), pp. 200–204.

10. *The Works of Geoffrey Chaucer* (Cambridge, Mass.: Harvard University Press, 1957), p. 387.

11. See Derek Brewer, *Chaucer in His Time* (London: Nelson, 1964), pp. 226–30.

12. *Liber Albus*, p. 427.

13. *Ibid.*, p. 54. Among the "ancient books" were obviously Fitzstephen's description of London and Geoffrey's *Historia*.

14. (Abbeville, 1468), I, Sig. A viii recto. I owe this reference to Prof. John V. Fleming. On the tradition of a moral cause for the fall of Troy and on the relationship between Troy and Troilus suggested below, see John P. McCall, "The Trojan Scene in Chaucer's *Troilus*," *ELH*, XXIX (1962), 263–75.

15. See John P. McCall and George Rudisill, Jr., "The Parliament of 1386 and Chaucer's Trojan Parliament," *JEGP*, LVIII (1959), 276–88.

Clio and Venus:
An Historical View of
Medieval Love

JOHN F. BENTON
California Institute of Technology

To make a fresh start in the study of an established subject usually requires a difficult act of renunciation, to put aside, at least temporarily, the interpretations, assumptions, concepts, and sometimes even the vocabulary which have become accepted. The subject of love in the Middle Ages has long been treated by sensitive and influential authors. If we are now to avoid some of the difficulties they have left us, I must initially ask my audience to acquiesce in a willing suspension of preconceptions and to imagine for a time that Stendahl had not in 1822 presented his reading of Provençal literature in his *Essai sur l'amour*, that Gaston Paris had not introduced the term and concept of "courtly love," *amour courtois*, in his study of Lancelot in *Romania* in 1883, and that C. S. Lewis had never written *The Allegory of Love*. If you are willing to go along with me in this renunciation, perhaps you will also put aside for a bit a few other works, including the chapter on "Courtly Love" in Sidney Painter's *French Chivalry* and Denis de Rougemont's *L'amour et l'occident*, published in the United States as *Love in the Western World* and in Great Britain as *Passion and Society*.[1]

Most work on love in the Middle Ages has been based on literature, particularly lyric poetry and romances, works which may often be difficult to understand, or at least are subject to controversial interpretations. Fortunately, there is ample material for an elementary knowledge of medieval love, marriage, and sexual mores in more secure historical sources. Spiritual and canonistic writing, medical treatises, penitentials, letters, chronicles, law codes, court cases and much more provide a solid basis for understanding literary works. So let us begin with what Clio can tell us of Venus in her medieval garb.

In the first feudal age, when the authority of both church and secular government was very weak, marriage could be seen simply as a personal contract, enforced by the families of the people involved.[2] Financial considerations were always of prime importance. The Germanic tradition of marriage by capture *(raptus)* appears in the penalty to be paid to the father or other guardian who had lost his property, and ordinarily a legal marriage began with a financial contract between the two families. If there was a reason for separation and acceptable financial arrangements could be made, the marriage might end with a divorce by mutual consent.[3] Although in practice many marriages may have been based on the free choice of both parties, there was almost no legal authority to enforce the Romano-canonical principle that consent makes a marriage *(consensus facit nuptias)*. We may be sure that the weak commonly experienced abduction, repudiation, and uncontrolled brutality.

In contrast, the second feudal age delineated by Marc Bloch was a time of institutionalization. The same social and intellectual movements which brought increasing order to the ties of government, or which led to the numbering, clarification, and explanation of the sacraments, also brought greater order, principle, and control into marriage. Without idealizing the next stage of medieval marriage or ignoring the personal hardships which followed from laws based on an unstable mixture of scriptural injunctions, established customs, equity, and concern for human needs, it is still clear that the institution of marriage was greatly strengthened, if not truly recreated, by the legal and social revival of the late eleventh and twelfth centuries. The consent of both parties, clearly expressed, was considered essential; marriage could follow rape only if the woman desired;[4] and there were courts to protect the rights of the weak and to limit the excesses of the brutal.

Although the ecclesiastical prohibition of divorce made the termination of an unfortunate marriage difficult, the problem of unilateral repudiation was greatly reduced. In short, for the average bride the institution of marriage improved markedly in the twelfth and thirteenth centuries.

The preference for celibacy over marriage is so prominent in medieval religious writing that it is easy to overlook the underlying assumption that marriage was both normal and desirable for most people. Of course, St. Paul's teaching that marriage provides a remedy for a common weakness of the flesh appears regularly in dispensations to marry lest worse things ensue. But in addition to this apostolic concession, the influence of family alliances, property rights, desire for legitimate offspring, social status, and the prospect of companionship all worked to make marriage attractive to the participants. We cannot know how much our medieval ancestors looked forward to what we would call a satisfying personal relationship—surely much less than do modern Americans. But the ideal of marriage, if not always the reality, was that there should be love between the spouses.

The Epistle to the Ephesians, attributed to St. Paul throughout the Middle Ages, contains the exhortation (5:25), "Husbands, love your wives," and the prayer that the bride "be as loveable as Rachel to her husband" was included in the early medieval wedding service. In the twelfth century Hugh of St. Victor, one of the most sympathetic commentators on marriage, stressed that the sacrament of marriage was instituted before the Fall and from the beginning was based on mutual love. St. Thomas Aquinas called the affection between husband and wife "the greatest friendship" (*maxima amicitia*), and following Aristotle said it was based on delight in the act of generation, utility in domestic life, and, in some cases, the virtue of the husband and wife.[5]

But if it was expected that marriage should produce love, what of love before marriage? To raise the question in this way shows how the word love stretches to cover many different situations, including the settled affection of a married couple established in their intimacy, what Aquinas calls friendship, and the passionate desire for union of a couple whose physical relations are unconsummated or unsanctioned. What we are asking here is if it was common for a couple to marry after being attracted to each other by passion. A frequent answer is that there was no place in medieval society for premarital familiarity, or for passion to lead to marriage. No doubt in many cases this generalization is true. Although by law no marriage was valid until the partners were old enough to consent and had done so, and a considerate or prudent parent would not choose a spouse repugnant to his child, marriages were commonly arranged, often when the partners were mere infants, and the marital confrontation of frightened children must have been all too common. We are given a glimpse of such unhappiness in a decretal of Clement III which tells of a girl who was given in marriage by her step-father at the age of eleven, although she was "unwilling and objecting," and who ran away to another man after a year and a half. The pope ruled that the girl should be returned to her husband, since by living with him for so long "she seems to have consented" to the marriage.[6]

But the picture of marriage as loveless initially and perhaps forever is not completely representative, and is distorted in part because our records are almost entirely of marriages which came into court. Still for the later middle ages ecclesiastical registers reveal much premarital passion in a wealth of "breach of promise" and clandestine marriage suits.[7] And if we look, we can find some evidence of marriages following the attraction of carnal passion in the twelfth and thirteenth centuries. As a witness let us call Philip the Fair's *bailli* from Beauvaisis, Philippe de Beaumanoir, who reports: "When a man has congress with a woman outside the bond of marriage and so has a child, and he marries her after the children are born or when she is pregnant, if the children are placed beneath the sheet which is customarily put over those who are ceremonially married in Holy Church, the legitimacy of the children should not be questioned, since they were placed there with the father and mother celebrating the marriage. . . . And through the grace which Holy Church and custom concede to such children, it happens often that their fathers marry their mothers out of pity for the children, so that less harm comes of it."[8]

As Professor Jackson points out in his paper, this explanation applies very well to the story of Rivalen and Tristan. And in real life, these so-called "mantle-children," heirs who were legitimated *"sub pallio,"* appear as a common problem in the laws and court cases of Germany, France, and England, and are proof enough of the existence of carnal love before marriage. The public attitude of the English nobility toward these fruits of careless love is shown by the action of the English baronage assembled at the Council of Merton in 1236, who resoundingly denied Bishop Grosseteste's proposal that common law should treat "mantle-children" as legitimate heirs. Love before marriage was familiar, and the barons did not approve of it.[9]

There should be no doubt that throughout the period we are considering some men chose wives they found physically and personally desirable, and women could presumably exercise some choice in how and to whom they seemed attractive. Among the causes of marriage Peter Lombard includes beauty, "which often inflames the soul with love."[10] At the same time that he advises against choosing a bride who can read, the author of *Urbain le Courtois* tells men not to marry for beauty.[11] The theme of the eventual marriage of lovers is common in medieval literature, more so, it seems to me, than that of adultery. Marrying for love was a good way to end a romance. Perhaps I may add, however, that even in literature love based on desire was not always assumed to be the ideal beginning to marriage and could be a source of trouble, as in the tale told by Chaucer's Franklin.[12]

Theoretical statements, literary examples, or exceptional cases did not overcome the social and economic pressure in the upper-classes to use marriage to join house to house and lay field to field. For the highly placed, the noble and the wealthy, arranged marriages remained the common pattern.[13] But for poorer people, often held back from early marriage by economic limitations, the personal choice of a partner based on familiarity and love could become increasingly routine. In 1484 Bernarde, daughter of a bourgeois of Troyes, told a neighbor that she was in love and had become engaged. The neighbor asked if she had the consent of her father. Bernarde replied that she didn't care about her father, that if he was upset by it he would calm down, and that several girls of better families than hers had married without parental consent and were very well off with their husbands.[14] Simple Bernarde! Her appeal to the precedent of families higher in the social scale was misplaced. She should have claimed she was setting the style of the future.

After discussing love in marriage and love before marriage, let us turn now to extra-marital love. This subject bulks so large in current literary history that it is desirable to take a close look at how adultery was actually treated in the Middle Ages. To begin with, both Roman law and the Germanic codes punished adulterers very severely. The penalty provided in the Theodosian Code (XI, 36, 4) was that the violators of marriage should be sewed in a leather sack and burned alive, but Justinian tempered this to give the woman a scourging and send her to a nunnery, from which her husband might release her if he chose (Nov. 134, c. 10).[15] The barbarian codes often provide the penalty of death, or permit a father or husband to kill an erring daughter or wife, and a husband could kill his wife's seducer without incurring vendetta. Writing to King Aethelbald of Mercia in the mid-eighth century, St. Boniface reported: "In Old Saxony, if a virgin defiles her father's house by adultery or if a married woman breaks the marriage tie and commits adultery, they sometimes compel her to hang herself, and then over the pyre on which she has been burned and cremated they hang the seducer." Such extreme penalties were, of course, not always invoked or even sought. The law code of King Aethelbert of Kent, written around 600, provides for a reasonable, if expensive, composition: "If a free man lies with the wife of a free man, he shall pay [the husband] his wergild and buy a second wife with his own money, and bring her to the other man's home."[16]

While these references show that adultery could have serious consequences, two considerations must be kept in mind. In both primitive Roman and early Germanic law, only women were bound by the chain of marriage, and a man was considered an adulterer only if he seduced a married woman. Although Christian law denounced this double standard and treated both partners to a marriage as equally responsible, in this area the church had little effect on the secular law of medieval Europe and even less on behavior. Even in the second feudal age it was considered altogether unusual for a husband to remain faithful to his wife. A chronicler remarked with surprise that Baldwin of Hainaut, who married the daughter of Henry and Marie of Champagne, loved his wife exclusively, "although it is rarely found in any man that he should cleave so much to one woman and be content with her alone."[17] The second consideration is that if a man were sufficiently powerful he could easily put himself above both law and private vengeance and seduce the wives of his neighbors or subjects with impunity. St. Boniface was, after all, writing the letter just quoted to reprove King Aethelbald for his adulteries, and William IX of Aquitaine felt free to boast humorously about his conquests.[18]

The differences which developed during the post-Carolingian period between northern and southern Europe in the judicial treatment of adultery are striking. In the southern lands of written law adultery continued to be treated as a capital crime, along with such offenses as homicide, bloodshed, theft, and rape. In some charters of franchise the lord had the right to confiscate all the adulterer's goods and the offender's body was at the lord's mercy. The more common penalty in southern France was that the offending couple should run or be paraded naked through the town or village, sometimes tied together shamefully; in some places this punishment could be avoided by paying a heavy fine. Unfortunately, very little material exists to show how strictly these penalties were enforced.[19] In the north the legal situation was much less rigorous, for adultery was ordinarily not tried in secular courts, but was an ecclesiastical offense.[20] Church courts rarely imposed heavy fines, the most severe penalty was usually scourging, and it seems to have been quite simple to avoid censure for a long time if not altogether. In the late twelfth century one English couple, living adulterously in the eyes of the church, had ten sons before Pope Celestine III imposed perpetual continence on them, a penalty he thought appropriate "as they are both advanced in years and by knowingly continuing so long in public adultery and perjury have disturbed the church by grave scandal."[21] In 1302 the court of Edward I, brought into the matter by a suit for dower, found that a couple had notoriously lived together in adultery, although they had certificates from the archbishop of Canterbury and the bishop of Chichester that they had cleared themselves of the charge of adultery by compurgation in court Christian. All that the secular court could do was to enforce the provision of the Second Statute of Westminister (1285) that a woman who deserted her husband to stay with a paramour should have no dower unless reconciled with her husband.[22]

Although adulterers might easily avoid serious punishment from a court, the tradition of private vengeance was so strong that violators of marriage still ran grave risks. In a letter of 857 which became part of Gratian's *Decretum*, Pope Nicolas I referred to a husband's right "according to secular law" to kill his adulterous wife. No doubt such extreme revenge was accepted in the first feudal age; chroniclers report that in about 1000 Count Fulk Nerra of Anjou burned his adulterous wife Elizabeth. Even in the late thirteenth century Beaumanoir notes that if a husband has publicly warned a man to stay away from his home and then finds him lying with his wife, he can with impunity kill both of them or the man alone, so long as he does it immediately in hot blood.[23]

In the second feudal age, however, the most extreme action taken against a wife was usually repudiation, as when Count William VIII of Montpellier put aside his wife Eudoxia, daughter of Emperor Manuel Comnenus. Churchmen viewed even this penalty as too severe. With respect to the case of William of Montpellier, Innocent III wrote in 1202, "although faithfulness to the marriage bed is one of the three goods of marriage, nevertheless its violation would not break the marital bond." Common custom was harsher. *Eructavit*, the translation and commentary on the 44th psalm dedicated to Countess Marie of Champagne, states as the custom of the world that when a woman deserts the love of her husband for another, either through sin or through a mistake, even though she fully repents her husband has no obligation to take her back and she would in fact be better off in the grave.[24]

Wives were usually treated more gently than their seducers. When Count Philip of Flanders suspected a young noble of adultery with the countess, he executed him by hanging him upside down down in a latrine, while his wife, heiress of Vermandois, was simply disgraced. Besides the possibility of death, a man who came between a husband and wife also ran the risk of mutilation, for the brutal vengeance suffered by Abelard was a common form of private revenge for attacks on the sanctity of the home.[25]

One form of adultery was considered iniquitous beyond all the rest, and that was the crime of a vassal who betrayed his lord. Adultery with the lord's wife was a form of treason. The eleventh-century customs of Barcelona call it "the greatest felony," along with compassing the death of the lord or his legitimate son or taking a castle and refusing to return it. Death remained the accepted punishment for such treason; Ramon Vidal, a Catalan poet of the early thirteenth century, vividly describes a lord's retainers setting out to kill as a traitor a vassal believed guilty of adultery with the lord's wife. In the greatest scandal of the reign of Philip the Fair, when two nobles were accused of adultery with the wives of Prince Louis and Prince Charles, the king had the young men castrated, dragged behind horses to the gallows and hanged, since they were (as one chronicler put it) "not only adulterers, but the vilest traitors to their lords."[26]

Instances like these should have been enough to destroy the idea that medieval troubadours roamed about the countryside advocating adultery and addressing suggestive songs, more or less thinly disguised, to the wives of the local lords, for a poor troubadour was certainly a vulnerable rival. The best proof that the lords of medieval Europe saw no threat in love songs, even when addressed to their wives, is that troubadours, trouvères, and minnesingers not only survived but made a living.[27] If Bernart de Ventadorn had really been intimate with Eleanor of Aquitaine and had left court because of Henry's jealousy, is it conceivable that he would have made public a song about it?[28]

Having reiterated how serious the consequences of adultery could be, I should also stress the toleration of it which was so commonly found in some circles of medieval society. As we have seen, if a husband did not take action himself, adultery often went unpunished and perhaps even uncensured. Medieval literature can be quite complacent about adultery, as in the *fabliaux* stressing the foolishness of the cuckold or in the song attributed to the Countess of Die, in which a lady sings to her knight that she has "a strong desire to hold you in place of my husband, as long as I have your promise to do all that I would like."[29] Of course adultery was offensive to anyone who valued the purity of noble bloodlines or took his (or her) religion seriously. But there were also nobles who shared Aucassin's preference to go to hell with the knights who die in tourneys and fine wars and with the beautiful, courteous ladies who have two or three lovers along with their lords. For such people the issue of adultery was not morality but honor, and their major concern was who wore the horns. For every woman who betrayed her husband there was a man who had made a conquest; the interest of the seducer was, of course, not in preventing adultery but in protecting his own honor through the virtue of his wife. In short, to make light of sexual adventures and adultery was more acceptable in the camp of William IX than in the sewing circle of his wife. We should not assume that a literature of loose morals was something which medieval women imposed on their men.

The great difficulties for modern understanding of medieval society have not been raised, however, by writings which express a light attitude toward adultery, but by those great works of literature like *Tristan* and *Lancelot* which treat it as a very serious subject indeed. An example of casual looseness is Ulrich von Zatzikhoven's *Lanzelet*, derived from an Anglo-Norman story of the twelfth century. In this version the hero, able both on the battlefield and in bed, has affairs with four women, ending with marriage to one, but he carefully stays away from King Arthur's wife. According to the mores of the time, this hero lived up to knightly expectations. The romance told by Chrétien de Troyes is in direct, and I think deliberate, contrast to this loose tale; Chrétien has gone out of his way to describe behavior he could be sure the courtly audience would condemn. In Chrétien's story the knight who rides in a shameful cart is no casual lover, but one who betrays his lord. In terms of the conventional standards of the court of Champagne, Chrétien's Lancelot was not more of a hero for loving Guinivere, but a felon. If we find Lancelot a sympathetic figure because he was guided by love rather than reason, it is because modern attitudes differ from medieval ones in ways Chrétien could not foresee.[30]

I am therefore in agreement with Professor Robertson that Chrétien wrote courteously of Lancelot and left him locked in a tower, rather than condemning him explicitly, not because he found his behavior admirable but because he was writing in the medieval tradition of irony. This literary device was summed up simply by an early thirteenth-century teacher of grammar and rhetoric at Bologna, Boncompagno of Signa, in a definition which deserves a place at the beginning of every edition of *Lancelot*.[31]

"Irony is the unadorned and gentle use of words to convey disdain and ridicule. If he who expresses irony may be seen, the intention of the speaker may be understood through his gestures. In the absence of the speaker, manifest evil and impure belief indict the subject. . . . Hardly anyone can be found who is so foolish that he does not understand if he is praised for what he is not. For if you should praise the Ethiopian for his whiteness, the thief for his guardianship, the lecher for his chastity, the lame for his agility, the blind for his sight, the pauper for his riches, and the slave for his liberty, they would be struck dumb with inexpressible grief to have been praised, but really vituperated, for it is nothing but vituperation to commend the evil deeds of someone through their opposite, or to relate them wittily."

Up to this point I have been discussing love that has an obvious connection with sexuality, and this was hardly the only aspect of love which was important in the Middle Ages. Augustine, who thought there was something inherently evil about all carnal desire, explained carefully that in Scripture the word *amor* is used both of a good affection and of an evil love. As he put it in his influential *City of God*, "The right will is, therefore, good love, and the wrong will is evil love." This idea of a division of love was commonplace in the twelfth century; as Hugh of St. Victor put it succinctly: "two streams flow from the single fount of love, cupidity and charity." In the next century Thomas Aquinas ponderously demonstrated that it was proper to distinguish between the love of friendship and the love of concupiscence.[32] Note that for St. Thomas, as we have already seen, delight in the act of generation could increase friendship in marriage. Sexual pleasure in marriage, fully consonant with reason, was a good thing. In short, Aquinas followed Aristotle in arguing that taking pleasure from any reasonable and appropriate behavior was natural and desirable.[33]

The idea that "love," expressed reasonably and appropriately, is a good thing can be found throughout medieval society. In religious terms, every Christian should love his neighbor, and in feudal terms, vassal and lord and their families should be bound by love. According to a ninth-century manual, a vassal should "fear, love, worship, and cherish" the relatives of his lord. Neither Christian charity nor feudal love necessarily involved an emotional or passionate personal attachment. Roland says that Charlemagne loved his vassals for the blows they struck. Love could express a purely formal relationship, a political alliance, the deference of a vassal before his lord, the bond of all the monks in a monastery, including those who disliked each other. In these terms, which have nothing to do with sexual desire, it increased one's worth to "love" another worthy person, as it increased one's honor to "love" a person of higher status.[34]

These theoretical statements provide a background for understanding medieval poetry in which a courtly writer says that he loves his lady. For a troubadour, traveling from court to court and singing to many ladies, these songs probably did not imply an emotional commitment, even when expressed in terms which sound quite passionate to us. Contemporaries could assume that the singer of love songs was not necessarily courting a woman, but only being courteous. The troubadour Elias Cairels defended himself against a forward lady, who was perhaps the creature of his imagination, by saying, "If I have sung your praise, it was not for dalliance *(drudaria)*, but for the honor and profit which I expected from it, as a jongleur does with a lady of worth."[35]

The love of friendship could also include those kisses and embraces which were often a part of medieval greetings, for in courtly circles it could be accepted as reasonable and appropriate to kiss a lady, to give her presents, to declare that one had become a better man through her friendship.[36] Such behavior should not be hard for us to understand, nor should we assume that it was concupiscent. If today a professor kisses his chairman's wife, or better yet the wife of a dean, gives her a present on her birthday, and treats her in a courteous fashion, no one need assume that he is not practicing "friendly love." If we today can distinguish between friendship and carnality, we should assume that medieval people could too. Of course, it is quite possible for a person to use the language of friendship with cupidinous desires in his heart. The danger of cupidity masquerading as proper love was the subject of a long discussion between the knight of La Tour Landry and his wife as to whether their daughters should court and kiss, and the hypocrisy of seduction provides much of the humor of the treatise on love by Andreas Capellanus.[37]

May I add in passing that since the lovers in Andreas' book were consistently unsuccessful, he can hardly have intended his work as a manual of seduction. What then was the purpose of his work? Perhaps we can judge from the view of Peter the Chantor, head of the school of moral philosophy at Paris at the end of the twelfth century. Peter was asked about the art of love, whether about Ovid's work in particular or the genre is not clear. He replied that "the art itself is good but its use is evil." The next question was then "does not he who teaches the amatory art use it and sin mortally?" To which it was replied that the teacher "does not use it but transmits it. He who corrupts women by its means uses it. Nevertheless, the teacher transmits it, not for use but as a warning."[38]

This part of the discussion may be summarized by attempting to be precise about terms. According to one group of medieval theorists there were two forms of love, one of which was reasonable and appropriate to the persons involved, could be practiced without sin or social affront, and was in fact good in itself; Aquinas called this the "love of friendship" and the troubadour Guillem Montanhagol said that chastity proceeds from it *(d'amor mòu castitatz)*. There was a second form of loving directed toward the satisfaction of carnal desire, which Aquinas called the love of concupiscence and the troubadour Marcabru termed false friendship *(fals' amistat)*. In theory love was the source of both branches, but they were very different in their ends and in their expression. We therefore create nothing but confusion for ourselves if we apply one technical term, other than the ambiguous word "love," to both forms of loving.[39] In particular I see no justification for combining aspects of one form of loving with aspects of the other and calling our creation "courtly love." While some authors wrote ambiguously about love, the literature I have read does not convince me that medieval people themselves inadvertently confused the categories and could not tell the difference between love which was concupiscent and that which was not. It seems to me that medieval authors and audiences enjoyed ambiguity in literature, not because they felt it reflected a basic ambiguity in the universe or the heart of man, but because their natural tendency was to think in very rigid categories. As the *Chanson de Roland* puts it (l. 1015), "Pagans are wrong and Christians are right."

An example of a passage in which some modern critics believe there is a combination of the two forms of love is that humorous dialogue by Andreas Capellanus in which a lover explains to a virgin that "pure love" proceeds "as far as kissing on the mouth and embracing and bashful contact with the nude lover, omitting the final solace."[40] The omission of the final act of Venus, which Andreas assumes may easily be reached later, preserves virginity, but it does not make the love chaste. How could anyone think it would? To do so requires the expectation that it is easy and in fact common for two naked lovers embracing together to avoid intercourse if one of them, presumably the woman, will only call a halt, thereby sublimating sexual desire into a spiritual relationship. This idea could be held in the Victorian period, when it was widely assumed that decent women did not enjoy sexual relations, and it still seems to linger on today. But it is a view which clashes with medieval views on physiology and the sexuality of women.

The medical theory inherited from antiquity was that both men and women are driven toward intercourse by their physiology. Women were thought to produce a seed (or *menstruum*) which collects in the womb and which gives rise to increasing sexual desire as it accumulates. Menstruation was considered the equivalent of a man's *pollutio* and to provide periodic relief; during pregnancy, when the *menstruum* was retained to nourish the fetus, a woman was at the peak of her sexual desire. Although medical treatises are imprecise in their terminology, orgasm seems to have been the indication of the emission of the female seed in intercourse. In any case, a woman's emission of seed, necessary for conception, was thought to be as pleasurable as that of a man; in fact, women were said to have twice the pleasure in intercourse as men, for they not only expelled seed but received it.[41] The natural consequence of this belief was the conclusion that a woman who conceived had taken pleasure in intercourse. Complacently, male judges denied any suit for rape brought by a woman who had become pregnant from the assault.[42] This theory of physiology explains the one strong area of medieval sexual egalitarianism. Since the sexual needs of women were thought to be as compelling as those of men, if not more so, a husband had as much responsibility to pay the marriage debt to his wife as she to him. The only woman who was not thought eager for sexual relations with someone was the unawakened woman. A woman would consequently choose a poor lover rather than have no man at all; as William IX put it, if denied wine anyone "would drink water rather than die of thirst." When contemplating other men's wives, as Duke William did, a man could take pleasure in this thought. But a man who brought back to his home the views of that bitter treatise, the *Quinze Joyes de Mariage*, must have viewed with horror the unquenchable sexuality of his wife.[43]

Since the force of sexuality was so compelling for both man and woman, it would be hard for chaste love to be just a little bit carnal. Frustrated desire was not thought preferable to satisfaction, for the natural end of desire was intercourse.[44] If carnal lovemaking stopped short of that goal, it was probably because the woman was a virgin, a state not likely to remain permanent if she found caressing pleasant enough. What preserved friendly love was virtue, aided by God's grace, or at least a sense of proper behavior. In a humorous song Daude de Pradas tells us that he divides his love in three. He has a lady from whom he receives small gifts and an occasional kiss; he loves her in order to increase his worth. He also likes to visit an honest virgin *(francha piucella)* who lets him kiss her cheek and doesn't jump up when he squeezes her breast. And finally, once or twice a month he beds down with a girl who works for wages, in order to learn what she knows of the game of love.[45] Daude could tell what was appropriate with each woman, and we should be careful to maintain his distinctions in our literary criticism.

Neither chaste nor cupidinous love has any direct or necessary connection with Catharism or other medieval heresies. The love of friendship was an expression of feudal or Christian values. The Cathars condemned Christian sexual morality and advocated a sexual purity far more rigorous than that actually found in Christian society; as a thirteenth-century Cathar ritual puts it, "Chastity places a man next to God."[46] There is, of course, no theoretical bar to thinking that some troubadours who celebrated chaste love were Cathars. Some southern French nobles were Cathars and many were sympathetic to at least some aspects of the religion. But admiring sexual purity was not peculiar to Cathars, and to assume that a poet advocating chastity was a heretic would be equivalent today to assuming that anyone advocating racial justice is a Communist.

The other side of the coin is that Cathars, opposed on religious grounds to procreation, were thought by their adversaries to have a stronger bar against generation than sexual activity itself. It may well be that some Cathars practiced sodomy and other non-generative sexual acts, but if they did, they kept it to themselves as best they could and did not write songs about it.[47] And a person did not have to be a Cathar to wish to avoid conception; various contraceptive devices, potions and practices were known and used throughout medieval Europe. All the same, contraception was not, as far as I can tell, the subject of any courtly literature.[48]

Catharism has been overrated as an influence on the sexual mores of medieval Europe. Publicly the Cathars preached sexual purity, but they were of course not alone in this. If they had an effect on most European Christians, it was probably to make it more difficult to be an advocate of chastity. Sometime in the 1180's the canon Gervase of Tilbury, then in the service of the archbishop of Reims, came upon a girl in a vineyard and, in the words of the man to whom he told the story, "courteously spoke to her at length of lascivious love." To these blandishments the girl replied, "Good young man, God doesn't wish me to be your lover or that of any man, since if I should lose my virginity and my flesh should once be corrupted, without doubt I should fall irredeemably into eternal damnation." Gervase immediately realized that she was a Cathar and began to reason with her. When the archbishop rode up he had the girl arrested and taken to Reims, where she was tried for heresy. When she refused to recant, she was burned at the stake, and died a martyr's death.[49]

This example of the treatment of a virtuous young woman raises the question of what effect the canons of courtesy had on the status of women. It is widely assumed that the twelfth century marks the beginning of a new period in the improvement of the social status of women. Of course, for the average person, man or woman, life in 1300 was more prosperous and more secure than it had been in 1000, and for the upper classes it was vastly improved. And, as we have seen, the institution of marriage itself was strengthened. But these changes do not mean that the position of women had improved relative to that of men. If one judges by juridical status, the legal ability to inherit and administer property and bequeath it by will, to bring a suit in a court of law, to avoid remarriage if widowed, it is hard to see that the position of noble women improved between the first feudal age and the second, and Lady Stenton can even argue that for English women it went down after 1066.[50]

Why should one expect an improvement in status for women from a social code in which a man increased his honor by being polite? According to one French *lai* the ladies of a court in Brittany raised the question of why men liked to attend tourneys, why they adorned themselves and dressed in new clothes, why they sent presents of jewels and rings and other treasures, why they were honest and debonair, why they refrained from doing evil, why they liked gallantry and hugging and kissing. The answer, the ladies concluded in French, was a three-letter word.[51] Courtesy was created by men for their own satisfaction, and it emphasized a woman's role as an object, sexual or otherwise. Since they did not encourage a genuine respect for women as individuals, the conventions of medieval chivalry, like the conventions of chivalry in the southern United States, did not advance women toward legal or social emancipation. When men ignored chivalry, women were better off. Who would trade the position of Njal's wife for that of Isolt?

In this long but still abbreviated study I have attempted an introductory historical treatment of medieval love based largely on sources other than poetry and romances. In it I have not attributed any significant influence to the Cathars, and have not found it necessary to mention the Arabs, who may have contributed to the forms of Provençal songs but are not needed to understand the sexual mores or ideals of Christian Europe.[52] In addition, I have found no evidence of a dramatic change in social or sexual behavior or outlook spreading through southern France like a plague, later to infect the north from a few centers like the court of Champagne or that of Eleanor of Aquitaine. Those changes in behavior I have noted occurred gradually, were moderate in their effect and can be understood as part of a general movement toward a more peaceful and better ordered society in the second feudal age. This paper attempts no systematic explanation of all medieval love literature, but the works I have mentioned seem to me consistent with Christian or feudal ideals, or with a society in which many people were not easily shocked by adultery but saw no reason to advocate it as a way of life for others. There was much discussion of love in various forms, and women were frequently honored by poets. Such poetry, we are told, increased the honor and profit of the singer, and in fact the service of ladies (which is hardly the same thing as the worship of women) does not seem to have significantly advanced their legal or social position. The second feudal age, like the first, remained a man's world.

Of course there were changes, and to see how literature and behavior acted on each other between 1100 and 1400 is a fascinating subject not attempted here. In treating it the greatest danger to avoid is that of working backward. There is, for instance, no doubt that in 1400 Charles VI founded a court of love, a serious literary and courtly assembly, but the existence of such a court should not lead us to think that the courts of love described by Andreas Capellanus were anything but humorous figments of his imagination.[53] As an example of the problem of historical perspective, let us take up a specific question. At the end of the Middle Ages a noble could depict himself on a tournament shield on his knees before a lady. What then is the earliest point where we can find evidence, outside of poetry, that a noble felt that it added to his honor to present himself as kneeling before a lady? Marc Bloch includes in his *Feudal Society* a picture entitled "The Lover's Homage" of the seal of Raymond de Montdragon, which shows a knight kneeling before a lithe figure in long robes. Is this early thirteenth-century seal our earliest evidence? No, for the figure in the long robes is actually not a woman but a man in civilian dress.[54] I mention this picture, not to point out a minor error in the work of a historian I greatly admire, but because it illustrates so well a familiar process. We see so often what we want to see, or expect to see, not what is there. Working backwards within the limits of a poorly defined concept could lead any historian to see a woman instead of a man.

Henry Osborne Taylor prided himself on writing two volumes on the sixteenth century without using the word "Renaissance," leading Charles Haskins to say of the forbidden term that "if it had not existed we should have to invent it." I have found the term "courtly love" no advantage in trying to understand the theory and practice of love in medieval Europe. It is not a medieval technical term. It has no specific content. A reference to "the rules of courtly love" is almost invariably a citation of Andreas'

De Amore, a work which I think is intentionally and humorously ambiguous about love. The study of love in the middle ages would be far easier if we were not impeded by a term which now inevitably confuses the issue. As currently employed, "courtly love" has no useful meaning, and it is not worth saving by redefinition. I would therefore like to propose that "courtly love" be banned from all future conferences.

Appendix

Definition of irony by Boncompagnus de Signa from his *Rhetorica antiqua* (c. 1215)[55]

P = Paris, Bibl. nat., ms. lat. 8654, fol. 6^r
M = Munich, Staatsbibliothek, Clm 23499, fol. 4^r
V = Vatican City, Archivio della Basilica di San Pietro, H. 13, fol. 9^v-10^r

Notula qua doctrina datur quid sit yronia et eius effectus.

Nota quod premissa narratio destinari potest etiam illi qui huc et illuc vagatur et studere contempnit, et dicitur hec species yronie in qua delinquens afficitur maiori pudore. Yronia enim est plana et demulcens verborum
5 positio cum indignatione animi et subsannatione. Verumtamen si videretur ille qui proponit yroniam, per gestus comprehendi posset voluntas loquentis. In absentia nempe manifestum delictum et immunda conscientia recipientem accusant. Gestus autem illorum qui subsannant et yronias proponunt subtiliter et utiliter in libro quem feci de gestibus et motibus corporum huma-
10 norum notavi. Ceterum vix aliquis adeo fatuus reperitur qui non intelligat si de eo quod non est conlaudetur. Nam si commendares Ethyopem de albedine, latronem de custodia, luxuriosum de castitate, de facili gressu claudum, cecum de visu, pauperem de divitiis, et servum de libertate, stuperent inenarrabili dolore laudati, immo vituperati, quia nil aliud est vituperium quam
15 alicuius malefacta per contrarium commendare vel iocose narrare. . . .

2 huc *om.* M	3	dicitur] quod *add.* V
4 efficitur M	9	quem] inquid V
11 si de—est] si non est de eo quod V		
11 conlaudetur] laudetur M, laudatur V		

Notes

1. To cite authors with whom I have occasion to disagree throughout the footnotes of this paper would be both invidious and unnecessary. The informed reader will have no difficulty in recognizing opposing views, and the beginner will find his way more directly to the sources. To make those sources as accessible as possible I have noted translations wherever I could. For several

37

helpful suggestions I owe thanks to Professors Elizabeth A. R. Brown, John W. Baldwin, and Thomas N. Bisson.

2. For quite different summary statements on medieval marriage see Gabriel Le Bras, s.v. "Mariage," *Dictionnaire de théologie catholique*, and Frederick Pollock and Frederic William Maitland, *History of English Law* (2nd ed.; Cambridge, Eng.: University Press, 1898), II, 364–99.

3. There are texts illustrating marriage contracts, divorce by mutual consent and a charter of composition for rape serving as a transfer of dowry in M. Thévenin, *Textes relatifs aux institutions privées et publiques aux époques mérovingienne et carolingienne* (Paris: A. Picard, 1887), #8, 17, 23, 41, 42, 48.

4. In the late twelfth century "Glanvill" maintained that men of good birth could not be forced into marriage by women of low estate, but Bracton in the next century permits this disparagement if the woman chooses it. See *The Treatise on the Laws and Customs of the Realm of England Commonly Called Glanvill*, ed. G. D. G. Hall (London: Nelson, 1965), Bk. XIV, 6, p. 176, and Henricus de Bracton, *De Legibus Angliae*, Rolls series, 70 (London: Longman, Trubner, 1878–1883), II, 491–93 (fol. 148).

5. *Liber Sacramentorum Romanae Aeclesiae*, ed. Leo C. Mohlberg, Rerum ecclesiasticarum documenta, Fontes, IV (Rome: Herder, 1960), Bk. III, 52, p. 210; Hugh of Saint Victor in Migne, *Patrologia latina*, CLXXVI, 314–15, trans. Roy J. Defarrari, *On the Sacraments of the Christian Faith* (Cambridge, Mass.: Mediaeval Academy of America, 1951), pp. 324-25; Aquinas, *In X libros ethicorum Aristotelis ad Nicomachum expositio*, Bk. VIII, 12, ed. Raimondo M. Spiazzi (3rd ed.; Turin: Marietti, 1964), p. 452, and *Summa Contra Gentiles*, Bk. III, 123–24, trans. by Vernon J. Bourke as *On the Truth of the Catholic Faith* (Garden City, N.Y.: Image Books, 1956), III, pt. 2, 147–52. Aquinas uses the term *amicitia* along with *amor* to avoid any possible confusion with the "love of concupiscence." Cf. F. J. E. Raby, "Amor and Amicitia," *Speculum*, XL (1965), 599–610.

6. *Decretales Gregorii IX*, IV, 1, 21, ed. E. Friedberg, II, 668–69. See also Jean Dauvillier, "Pierre le Chantre et la dispense de mariage non consommé," *Études d'histoire du droit privé offertes à Pierre Petot* (Paris: Librairie générale de droit et de jurisprudence, 1959), pp. 99–100.

7. Surprisingly little social history has been based on the voluminous records of ecclesiastical courts. The registers of the archdeacon's courts in England remain virtually untouched. For published French registers and a fruitful example of what can be done with them, see Jean-Philippe Lévy, "L'officialité de Paris et les questions familiales à la fin du XIVᵉ siècle," *Études d'histoire du droit canonique dédiées à Gabriel Le Bras* (Paris: Sirey, 1965), II, 1265–94. A second great body of material even more surprisingly neglected by those concerned with the society of Chaucer are the Year Books, of which Maitland wrote, "It will some day seem a wonderful thing that men once thought they could write the history of mediaeval England without using the Year Books." The quotation is cited by William C. Bolland, *A Manual of Year Book Studies* (Cambridge, Eng.: University Press, 1925), p. 84.

8. *Coutumes de Beauvaisis*, Bk. XVIII, 23, ed. Amédée Salmon (Paris: Picard, 1899), I, 295–96.

9. R. Génestal, *Histoire de la légitimation des enfants naturels en droit canonique* (Paris: École Pratique des Hautes Études, 1905), and Albert Weitnauer, *Die Legitimation des ausserehelichen Kindes im römischen Recht und in den Germanenrechten des Mittelalters*, Basler Studien zur Rechtswissenschaft, 14 (Basel: Helbing und Lichtenhahn, 1940).

10. *Sentences*, Bk. IV, 30, 3, in *Libri IV sententiarum* (2nd ed.; Quaracchi, 1916), II, 934. Peter considered beauty a less proper cause for marriage than making peace or reconciling enemies.

11. Ed. Paul Meyer, *Romania*, XXXII (1903), 72.

12. For anyone who took canon law seriously, the Franklin's Tale provided no model for a happy marriage. The condition to which Arveragus swore, which gave his wife license for adultery, came dangerously close to violating the canon *Si conditiones* in *Decr.*, IV, 5, 7, ed. Friedberg, II, 634. That one should not keep an illicit oath is set forth in II, 24, 18 (*ibid.*, p. 365).

13. On arranged marriages in the English upper classes in the sixteenth and seventeenth centuries see Lawrence Stone, *The Crisis of the Aristocracy, 1558-1641* (Oxford: Clarendon, 1965), pp. 594-612.

14. Aube, arch. dép., G 4184, fol. 306ᵛ, analyzed in the *Inventaire sommaire, série G* (Troyes-Paris, 1896), II, 293. This testimony is an example of the material for social history in these registers. The irony of this case is that it came into court when Bernarde later denied that she was engaged and her fiancé requested that she be adjudged to him.

15. Percy E. Corbett, *The Roman Law of Marriage* (Oxford: Clarendon, 1930), pp. 145-46. There is an excellent translation of *The Theodosian Code* by Clyde Pharr (Princeton: Princeton University Press, 1952).

16. References to adultery in the Germanic laws are collected by Hermann Conrad, *Deutsche Rechtsgeschichte* (2nd ed.; Karlsruhe: C. F. Müller, 1962), I, 156; a good example is *The Burgundian Code*, trans. Katherine Fischer (Philadelphia: University of Pennsylvania Press, 1949), p. 68, § 68 and p. 45, § 34, 1. For the quotations see *Die Briefe des heiligen Bonifatius und Lullus*, ed. Michael Tangl, MGH, Epist. sel., I (Berlin, 1916), #73, p. 150, trans. by C. H. Talbot in *The Anglo-Saxon Missionaries in Germany* (New York: Sheed and Ward, 1954), p. 123; and F. L. Attenborough, *The Laws of the Earliest English Kings* (Cambridge, Eng.: University Press, 1922), p. 9, § 31. On penalties throughout medieval Europe see J. R. Reinhard, "Burning at the Stake in Mediaeval Law and Literature," *Speculum*, XVI (1941), 186-209.

17. *La Chronique de Gislebert de Mons*, ed. Léon Vanderkindere (Brussels: Kiessling, 1904), pp. 191-92.

18. The song in which William tells of tupping the wives of Lords Guarin and Bernart 188 times is edited by Alfred Jeanroy, *Les Chansons de Guillaume IX*, Classiques français du moyen âge, 9 (2nd ed.; Paris: Champion, 1927), pp. 8-13 (P.-C., 183, 12). There is a lively translation by Hubert Creekmore, *Lyrics of the Middle Ages* (New York: Grove, 1959), pp. 41-43. Whether the people in the song were recognizable individuals cannot now be known. On William's "courtly" songs see Peter Dronke, "Guillaume IX and courtoisie," *Romanische Forschungen*, LXXIII (1961), 327-338.

19. Auguste Molinier in *Histoire générale de Languedoc* (new ed.; Toulouse, 1872-1905), VII, 211; Jean Ramière de Fortanier, *Chartes de franchises du Lauragais* (Paris: Sirey, 1939), p. 535, § 5. A thirteenth-century illustration in the custumal of Toulouse, Paris, Bibl. nat., ms. lat. 9187, fol. 30ᵛ, shows a tied couple preceded by a man with a trumpet.

20. In the late twelfth century Peter the Chanter noted that an injured husband who did not choose to kill an adulterer might bring him before a secular judge, but added that he had never seen such a case tried in a secular court. See Pierre le Chantre, *Summa de sacramentis et animae consiliis*, ed. Jean-Albert Dugauquier (Louvain-Lille: Éditions Nauwelaerts, 1954-), pt. III, 2, a, p. 351.

21. *Decr.* IV, 7, 5, newly edited by Walther Holtzmann and Eric W. Kemp, *Papal Decretals Relating to the Diocese of Lincoln in the Twelfth Century*, Lincoln Record Soc., 47 (Hereford: Hereford Times, 1954), pp. 60–61.

22. Pollock and Maitland, *History of English Law*, II, 395–96.

23. Gratian, C. XXXIII, qu. II, c. 6, ed. Friedberg, I, 1152; on Fulk see Pierre Daudet, *L'établissement de la compétence de l'Église en matière de divorce et de consanguinité* (Paris: Sirey, 1941), pp. 23–24; Beaumanoir, *Coutumes*, XXX, 102, ed. Salmon, I, 472–73.

24. Innocent's "Per venerabilem," *Decr.* IV, 17, 13, trans. by Brian Pullan, *Sources for the History of Medieval Europe* (Oxford: Blackwell, 1966), pp. 68–72; cf. *Decr.* III, 32, 15. *Eructavit*, ed. T. Atkinson Jenkins, Gesellschaft für romanische Literatur 20 (Dresden: Niemeyer, 1909), ll. 1577–94.

25. J. Johnen, "Philipp von Elsass, graf von Flandern," *Bulletin de la commission royale d'histoire [de Belgique]*, LXXIX (1910), 418–20; Pollock and Maitland, *History of English Law*, II, 485.

26. *Usatges de Barcelona*, ed. Ramon d'Abadal I Vinyals and F. Valls Taberner, Textes de dret catala, I (Barcelona, 1913), pp. 18–19, art. 40. Ramon Vidal's *Castía Gilos* is most recently printed in *Les Troubadours*, eds. René Nelli and René Lavaud (Paris: Desclée, De Brouwer, 1960–1966), II, 186–211; the lord had given the vassal in question a private residence, which is the meaning in l. 52 of *cassatz* < L. *casatus*. For the scandal of 1314 see Martin Bouquet, *Recueil des historiens des Gaules et de la France* (Paris, 1738–1904), XX, 609; XXI, 40; and XXI, 657.

27. This point was made over half a century ago, with all too little effect, by Stanislaw Stronski, *Le troubadour Folquet de Marseille* (Cracow: Académie des Sciences, 1910), pp. 61*–68*.

28. The song (P.-C., 70, 33) which Bernart addressed to Eleanor contains only conventional praise and no suggestion of improper conduct. "Per vos me sui del rei partitz" means simply that Bernart left the king because of her, and not specifically for her sake. If Bernart had fallen from the queen's favor and wished to return to court, what better song could he have written? See *The Songs of Bernart de Ventadorn*, ed. Stephen G. Nichols (Chapel Hill: University of North Carolina Press, 1965), pp. 138–40.

29. Gabrielle Kussler-Ratyé, "Les chansons de la comtesse Béatrix de Dia," *Archivum Romanicum*, I (1917), 173–74 (P.-C. 46, 4). Without some evidence of a particularly complacent Count of Die, the attribution of this song to any Countess of Die seems to me questionable.

30. *Lanzelet*, ed. K. A. Hahn (Frankfurt: Brönner, 1845), trans. and ed. by Kenneth G. T. Webster and Roger S. Loomis (New York: Columbia University Press, 1951); *Le chevalier de la charrette*, ed. Mario Roques (Paris: Champion, 1958), trans. by William Wistar Comfort in Chrétien de Troyes, *Arthurian Romances* (London: J. M. Dent, 1914).

31. Paris, Bibl. nat., ms. lat. 8654, fol. 6ʳ. The Latin text follows as an appendix. Cf. D. W. Robertson, Jr., *A Preface to Chaucer* (Princeton: Princeton University Press, 1962), pp. 448–52.

32. *City of God*, Bk. XIV, ch. 7; Hugh of St. Victor, Migne, *PL*, CLXXVI, 15, trans. as "The Nature of Love" in his *Selected Spiritual Writings* (London: Faber and Faber, 1962), p. 187; *Summa theologica*, First Part of the Second Part, qu. 26, art. 4. Cf. Ovid, *Fasti*, IV, 1.

33. For a full discussion see Josef Fuchs, *Die Sexualethik des heiligen Thomas von Aquin* (Köln: J. P. Bachem, 1949), pp. 21–30.

34. Edouard Bondurand, *L'Éducation carolingienne: le manuel de Dhuoda* (Paris: Picard, 1887), p. 103. See also the valuable semantic analysis of George F. Jones, *The Ethos of the Song of Roland* (Baltimore: Johns Hopkins Press, 1963), pp. 36–45.

35. P.-C. 133, 7, in Jules Véran, *Les Poétesses provençales* (Paris: A. Quillet, 1946), 152–57.

36. For a straightforward statement approving this form of love see *Le Breviari d'Amor de Matfre Ermengau,* ed. Gabriel Azaïs (Béziers-Paris: Delpech, 1862), II, 413–16, ll. 27291 ff., trans. into modern French by Nelli and Lavaud, *Troubadours,* II, 664–71.

37. *Le Livre du Chevalier de La Tour Landry,* ed. Anatole de Montaiglon (Paris: Jannet, 1854), pp. 246–65, trans. from a medieval English version by G. S. Taylor, *The Book of the Knight of La Tour Landry* (London: Verona Society, 1930), pp. 248–70; and Andreas Capellanus *De Amore,* ed. E. Trojel (Havniae: Libraria Gadiana, 1892), trans. John J. Parry, *The Art of Courtly Love* (New York: Columbia University Press, 1941).

38. Munich, Staatsbibliothek, Clm. 5426, fol. 163^r, to be published by Jean Albert Dugauquier as ch. 332 in the fourth volume of his edition of Pierre le Chantre, *Summa de Sacramentis.* Cf. Andreas, *De Amore,* p. 313 (Parry, p. 187).

39. *Les poésies de Guilhem de Montanhagol,* ed. Peter T. Ricketts (Toronto: Pontifical Institute of Mediaeval Studies, 1964), pp. 121–23 (P.-C. 225, 2); *Poésies complètes du troubadour Marcabru,* ed. J. M. L. Dejeanne, Bibl. mérid., 1st ser., 12 (Toulouse: E. Privat, 1909), Songs V and VI (P.-C. 293, 5 and 6). Fin' *amors,* meaning simply "true love," was not a technical term and was applied in various ways to both branches of love.

40. *De Amore,* p. 182 (Parry, p. 122). Cf. *De Amore,* pp. 264–65 (Parry, p. 164).

41. The epitome of thirteenth-century female sexology is *De secretis mulierum,* which exists in many early printed editions. For references see Lynn Thorndyke in *Speculum,* XXX (1955), 427–43. See also Trotula of Salerno, *The Diseases of Women,* trans. Elizabeth Mason-Hohl (Los Angeles: Ward Ritchie, 1940).

42. *Year Books of Edward II,* vol. V, Selden Soc., 24 (London, 1910), p. 111.

43. P.-C. 183, 4, ed. Jeanroy, p. 4; *Les Quinze joyes de mariage,* ed. Fernand Fleuret (Paris: Garnier, 1936), trans. Elisabeth Abbott, *The Fifteen Joys of Marriage* (New York: Orion, 1959).

44. The twelfth-century Bolognese canonist Huguccio does mention the practice of *amplexus reservatus* in his *Summa,* Bk. II, 13 as a way for a married man to avoid the venial sin of pleasure in ejaculation. Comparison of his text with the *De Amore* shows that Andreas was not writing of the same thing when he discussed *amor purus,* for this form of intercourse could not be called "vererecundus contactus" for a woman. Other twelfth and thirteenth-century canonists ignore this passage in Huguccio, quite probably not understanding what he means. See John T. Noonan, Jr., *Contraception: A History of Its Treatment by the Catholic Theologians and Canonists* (Cambridge, Mass.: Harvard University Press, 1965), pp. 296–99.

45. *Poésies de Daude de Pradas,* ed. A. H. Schutz, Bibl. mérid, 1st ser., 22 (Toulouse: Privat, 1933), pp. 69–74 (P.-C. 124, 2).

46. Antoine Dondaine, *Un Traité néo-manichéen du XIIIe siècle* (Rome: Institutum Historicum FF. Praedicatorum Romae, 1939), p. 162; cf. *ibid.,* pp. 125–27.

47. St. Bernard thought that the public profession of chastity and continence made by the dualist heretics was hypocritical, and considered that for a man to remain continually with a woman and not know her carnally would be mirac-

ulous. See *Sermones super Cantica,* LXV and LXVI in *S. Bernardi Opera,* ed. Jean Leclercq et al. (Rome: Editiones Cistercienses, 1957–), II, 172–88, esp. pp. 175–76 and 179–81. These sermons and the letter of Eberwin of Steinfeld *(P.L.,* 182, 676–80) which solicited them show that the heretics preached chastity, whether or not they practiced it.

48. On Catharism and contraception see Noonan, *Contraception,* esp. pp. 179–93.

49. Ralf of Coggeshall, *Chronicon Anglicanum,* Rolls series, 66 (London, 1875), pp. 121–24.

50. It is instructive to compare the later medieval chapters in *La Femme,* Recueils de la Société Jean Bodin, XII, pt. 2 (Brussels: Editions de la Librairie encyclopédique, 1962), with F. L. Ganshof's introductory essay on Frankish women. See also Doris M. Stenton, *The English Woman in History* (London: Allen and Unwin, 1957), p. 28.

51. "Lai du Lecheor," ed. Gaston Paris, *Romania,* VIII (1879), 65–66, ll. 71–92.

52. The contrast between the position of women in Moslem and Western European society is well illustrated by Jean Richard in *La Femme,* pt. 2, p. 387.

53. Theodor Straub, "Die Gründung des Pariser Minnehofs von 1400," *Zeitschrift für romanische Philologie,* LXXVII (1961), 1–14; on the courts mentioned by Andreas see my "Court of Champagne as a Literary Center," *Speculum,* XXXVI (1961), 580–82.

54. *La société féodale, la formation des liens de dépendance* (Paris: A. Michel, 1939), trans. L. A. Manyon (London: Routledge, 1961), plate IV; cf. Germain Demay, *Le Costume au moyen âge, d'après les sceaux* (Paris: D. Dumoulin, 1880). There is a picture of a fifteenth-century tournament shield in Joan Evans, *The Flowering of the Middle Ages* (London: Thames and Hudson, 1966), p. 142.

55. I am grateful to Professor Robert L. Benson for collating the Munich and Vatican manuscripts.

Dante:
Within Courtly Love
and Beyond

CHARLES S. SINGLETON
The Johns Hopkins University

I t seems appropriate to change my original title, "Beyond
Courtly Love," to one which will recognize that a very considerable part of Dante's literary work, chiefly his poetry of
course, falls quite *within* the confines of the courtly love tradition
—even if we may not always agree on just what those confines
were, and *are* (literary forms having a way of continuing to exist
in the present tense, over and over again, and perhaps taunting
the historian, as historian, by such a mysterious existence.) Dante,
in fact, was very much "within the tradition;" indeed, we may
fairly say that he made his debut within it. But, for purposes of
discussion, I shall look to a moment in his development as poet
when, having turned philosopher for the moment, he gives us a
certain terminology (as applying to the mode of courtly love and
to a mode beyond it) which may prove suggestive and fruitful to
this conclave, convened to discuss love and to distinguish *kinds* of
love. One term Dante can give us is *amoris accensio*, and the other
is *directio voluntatis*. But we had best recall the context of these
terms as he found occasion to use them.

In the *De vulgari eloquentia*, Dante concerns himself, first of all,
with language as such, with the nature of language and its particular history with man (beginning, of course, with Adam and at-
tending at once to what happened anent a certain overweening

43

construction project at Babel—and where else, if we are medievalists, *should* we begin?). But Dante manages, for all that *ab ovo* beginning, to come rapidly down to those languages we commonly term Romance, though not before he has made a passing effort to classify languages universally, according (among other features) to their affirmative particle, to the way they say "yes;" and accordingly, as all here will recall, he comes into focus on the Romance languages as being those of *oïl*, *oc* and *sì*. And coming to these, then, as *literary* languages (one suspected *that* was his interest, from the title of his treatise), as languages refined by poets (*trilingues doctores* as he terms them in this passage), he points out that these three languages agree by having in common the word *amor*—at which point in his discourse not only is the relevance of his developing argument evident enough to our conference here, but it is also clear that Dante is showing his hand, that his own particular interest in dealing with poetry in the vulgar tongue is to concern himself with the *literary* tradition of courtly love.

To this particular interest and concern he comes in the second Book of his treatise (which he left unfinished, and accordingly might be said to have abandoned *us* with our chosen subject) and to the two terms which I suggest may be of interest here—but let it be admitted forthwith that Dante is not about to abandon his very special predilection for the number three, even in this case, and that *his* terms are in that number three, and for the perfectly good reason that (as we all must know) we human creatures are 'animated' in a three-fold way. We have, technically speaking, three 'souls' (yet these are *one*, of course). And since the courtly, illustrious, cardinal, and curial vernacular should concern itself only with the most worthy of subject-matters, it follows that we should consider carefully what these might be, in accordance with our 'three-fold' constitution as human beings:

Ad quorum evidentiam sciendum est, quod sicut homo tripliciter spirituatus est, videlicet vegetabili, animali et rationali, triplex iter perambulat. Nam secundum quod vegetabile quid est, utile querit, in quo cum plantis comunicat; secundum quod animale, delectabile, in quo cum brutis; secundum quod rationale, honestum querit, in quo solus est, vel angelice nature sociatur. Per hec tria quicquid agimus agere videmur. Et quia in quolibet istorum quedam sunt maiora, quedam maxima, secundum quod talia, que maxima sunt maxime pertractanda videntur, et per consequens maximo vulgari.

Sed disserendum est, que maxima sint. Et primo in eo quod est utile: in quo, si callide consideremus intentum omnium querentium utilitatem, nil aliud quam salutem inveniemus. Secundo, in eo quod est delectabile: in quo dicimus illud esse maxime delectabile quod per preciosissimum obiectum appetitus delectat; hoc autem venus est. Tertio, in eo quod est honestum: in quo nemo dubitat esse virtutem. Quare hec tria, Salus videlicet, Venus et Virtus, apparent esse illa magnalia que sint maxime pertractanda, hoc est ea que maxime sunt ad ista, ut armorum probitas, amoris accensio, et directio voluntatis.[1]

Thus it is that we come to distinguish the three *magnalia* which are worthy of the illustrious vulgar tongue that poets, *trilingues doctores* that they are, have fashioned: *salus, venus, virtus* are their three names; and the corresponding poetic endeavors which relate to them, and may also stand as names for *literary* subject-matters, are the three we have just heard: *armorum probitas, amoris accensio,* and *directio voluntatis.* Whereupon Dante also tells us just which poets have excelled in these subjects in Provençal on the one hand, and in Italian on the other. The passage is familiar to us all. In *arma* the prize must go to Bertran de Born among the Provençals—whereas, among the Italians, none as yet has excelled in this subject. In *venus* or *amoris accensio,* Arnaut Daniel must be awarded the crown of excellence, and among the Italians, Cino da Pistoia. In *rectitudo* or *virtus* it is Girault de Bornehl who receives the palm, and among the Italians it is "Cino's friend."

ACCENSIO AMORIS

Dante is scarcely famous for his modesty, and there can be no doubt at all who "Cino's friend" is. Here, then, we have Dante classifying himself in the lyric tradition, and evidently classifying himself *beyond* (and above) the poetry of courtly love, for that poetry is surely, and centrally, the poetry that deals with *venus:* wherein Cino excels. But he, Dante, is a poet of *rectitudo,* his concern is with *directio voluntatis.*

In distinguishing these "prize-winners" in each case, Dante cites by *capoverso* the poem whereby each poet can, presumably, claim the prize. Thus, for Cino, in evidence of his high merit, he cites the *canzone*, "Digno sono eo de morte." This composition is extant and, were there time here, might justify our reading and careful consideration, it being Dante's choice of the *supreme* poem of the courtly love tradition (among the Italians, at least). But, for present purposes, I shall simply report that, in Cino's poem, the poet tells his lady that he is worthy of death because he has stolen Love from her eyes—so stealthily that she was unaware of it. It was great and foolish daring on his part to do this, and then to reveal the fact to her. And now this Love that he has so stolen from her is his undoing and death, and he constantly makes lament over this. But his Lady should not deign to concern herself with this cruel fact; and moreover the poet is resigned to death and consents to do battle with death. But would his Lady please forgive him his initial act of *hybris*, at least, may compassion bring her to this? It is a noble act to show pardon, when one is in a position to do vengeance.

Cino's prize poem in *venus*, in *amoris accensio* has, clearly, all the conventional trappings of the cult of courtly love, particularly as that cult had developed with poets on the Italian scene. Here is the familiar god of love, here is *madonna*, high-placed and cruel, here on the part of the poet are the tears and entreaties, here are the prayers for forgiveness. In short, we must recognize that Dante has chosen well in offering this as the most excellent example of poetry in the manner of *amoris accensio*. One could scarcely find a more representative example. It has all the elements.

But, of course, all readers of the passage we have quoted from the *De vulgari* will naturally wonder why Dante gives the prize to Cino in the manner of *venus* rather than to himself (apart from the fact that it would hardly be seemly for Dante to award himself *two* prizes). Had Dante himself not excelled in the poetry of courtly love? We have only to think of the extant corpus of his lyrics, all belonging unmistakably to that tradition, to increase our wonder here. Where else does the *Vita Nuova* itself begin, if not exactly *within* the cult of courtly love? And by the way, if I may at this point be permitted an aside, to whatever serious *social* historian may happen to be in our midst, I can assure him that we *do*

46

have the replies to the first sonnet of the *Vita Nuova*, replies *per le rime*, from Guido Cavalcanti and others, so that the *social* reality of this cult of courtly love in Florence, in Dante's time, is firmly attested by documentary evidence: courtly love, as practised by poets, *did* exist, then and there.

Guido, and Dante, and others, did *play* at courtly love. No serious historian of literature doubts this. Yet I venture to under-score the verb *play* because it has sometimes seemed to me that some scholars among us who have concerned themselves with our theme, "the *meaning of courtly love*," have allowed themselves to forget that it *was* all play. And this is the more surprising, because literary scholars presumably would know, as a kind of primal truth in the profession that, of course, all poetry is play, that all art-forms are play; and that we as readers or listeners are quite out of focus on what is supposed to be the very object of our interest if we forget this. But, curiously enough, there have been those who have found a special problem in the matter of courtly love and its *meaning*, as if we somehow cannot allow that good Chris-tians, Christians who know that there is only one God of Love, could play with a convention of *venus* that had, as a central figure, either a *god of love* in no way identifiable with the God of Love of the Christian faith, or else, at the center, had a woman, *midons*, enthroned and worshipped in his stead (or had, more commonly, *both* figures). Therefore, it is scandalous, indeed un-thinkable, that Christian poets should ever have entered into such a cult (and the Bishop of Paris *did* in fact think so); and accord-ingly, we must give another reading to this matter of courtly love, and so forth. But whenever (if ever again) we allow ourselves to get out of focus in this matter of courtly love, then I make bold to recommend, as antidote, the book by Huizinga[2] that will always come to mind in this regard, that we let Huizinga remind us that *play* belongs to the human spirit, and even to Christians as mem-bers of the human race; that Christians *have* found ways, after all, of playing *to one side of* (as *play* must do if it is to be play), or *out-from-under*, the Christian cult; perhaps we should say, to one side of the Christian's central and overriding concern for the sal-vation of his soul—which concern is the "serious business" of life, with respect to which *play* is recognizable as such, for *play* be-comes possible only if there *is* the "serious" whereby it can exist as

47

the "playful." Or perhaps, in this particular regard, it might suffice to remind ourselves that such a thing as *carnival* did and does exist, Carnival followed by Lent and repentance: a carnival time followed by lenten time, and therefore clearly marked off as being "a time." Carnival is, or was, a traditional play-time for Christians, a kind of *playground;* and, in fact, has some of the trappings of courtly love (though, heaven forbid, we shall not confuse the two): Carnival has its "god," who is a god of *fun,* be he called Bacchus or "bella giovinezza," and carnival has its poetry too (not very good poetry, let it be admitted), its *canti carnascialeschi* on the Italian scene, all quite lewd in nature, all constructions in obscene *double entendre,* for the most part; and carnival also has its theater, carnival being the time in which the revived comedies of Plautus could be performed, or an original *Mandragola.* In short, carnival was a time for "transferring oneself" out of the Christian cult, into another cult which was clearly and openly a denial of the true faith. This recalls a famous reflexive verb, *trasferirsi,* in that most famous letter of Machiavelli's about how he spent his evenings writing about another pagan time and cult when men were strong, all quite in contradiction with the "true way [i.e. the Christian way] of life."

Carnival was all good "Christian fun," and only *fun* in being the fun of *Christians.* To be sure, a Savonarola could always come along and rather sternly disapprove, with bonfires of vanities, and hymns in place of carnival songs; but then it might not go very well with him, finally, for all his pious intentions.

The cult of courtly love has its rules, like any game: a god of love, a *madonna,* cruelty, and mercy, and so forth, all the elements of Cino's "prize poem." *Amoris accensio:* Dante knew very well whereof he spoke, for he had played that game with all the seriousness that he, as poet, could put into it. Only subtract the *Vita Nuova,* the *Convivio,* the *Divine Comedy,* from the corpus of Dante's poetry (and what a subtraction!) and most of what remains is a poetic production that is unmistakably in the tradition with which we, at this conference, are chiefly concerned. Indeed, did we not have the narrative frame of the *Vita Nuova* to arrange the chosen poems in a sequence and meaning which removes some of them from being a part of the poetry of courtly love as we commonly understand that, then we should also have a goodly number of the poems of the *Vita Nuova* to add to the total corpus of Dante's lyrics written in the style of *amoris accensio.* Nor is that all. If we had extant *only* such a *corpus* of poetry by Dante, we should indeed wonder what he could possibly have meant by awarding the prize in that style to Cino; neither should we understand what he could possibly have meant in terming himself a poet of *directio voluntatis* rather than of *amoris accensio.* For only by having the *Vita Nuova,* the *Convivio,* and the *Commedia,* do we understand what *directio voluntatis* can mean as a poet's program, as his working principle.

DIRECTIO VOLUNTATIS

Having the *Commedia* in its entirety, as we do, nothing becomes easier to determine than what *directio voluntatis* can mean, as a poet's guideline, as his "poetics" or general statement of purpose. Here, of course, we have the advantage of hindsight, which Dante himself, when he classified himself under such a heading, did not have. Indeed by then he may not have begun, he may not even have conceived the *Commedia* as such. There at the end of the *Vita Nuova,* to be sure, is the resolve to write of his lady (in the style of *loda*) what had never been written of any woman. But was that resolution with him constantly in the hard years of exile? Apparently not, by his own confession and to judge from the charges of backsliding and defection which he causes Beatrice to make against him, when she comes to him at the summit of Mount Purgatory and stands in judgment on him. In those first years of Dante's exile there may well have been a *pargoletta* to distract him, and indeed more than one. Certainly, as a poet, he continued to play at the game of courtly love, with friend Cino, with Marquis Malaspina, and no doubt with others; and his *canzone* which (because of its *congedo*) we call *montanina,* and which is still entirely in the style of *amoris accensio,* can hardly have been written later than the time in which, in the *De vulgari,* he was classifying himself out of that tradition in the way we have seen.[3]

But in exile the poet had become a citizen of the world, with vast new horizons opening up for him; and indeed it is clear, even before his exile, that he had begun to think and work beyond the confines of courtly love, both as a poet and as a student of philosophy. Not that he abandons the cult of love, of *venus;* but a change of heart and of intellectual interests gradually prevails. Years later, in the *Paradiso,* he will have the Eagle say of the Trojan Ripheus that "he set all his love on rectitude" ("tutto suo amor là giù pose a drittura").[4] And this seems something which we in turn may fairly say of Dante himself, as he moves away from the game of courtly love toward broader vistas. *Drittura,* in the case of Ripheus, might also be understood as "justice," *inner* justice in his case, of course, which means *virtus* or *rectitudo.* And Dante's writing now, both the *canzoni* of the *Convivio* and his other poems, though continuing to be *love* poems, are about *drittura* in this sense of virtue and justice—so much so, indeed, so directly and seriously are they about virtue and justice that they almost cease to be *poetry* in any true sense of the word, and are simply more and more artfully-rhymed statements of "the truth," as he sees it, of *justice,* be it inner or social.

Yet *drittura* is not Dante's only theme in these years as he works beyond the earlier modes of courtly love; and to this the Lady whom he undertakes to celebrate in the *Convivio* attests most clearly. This *Banquet* is a feast of *Sapientia,* this lady whom he praises in such extremes is none other than Lady Philosophy herself, as known to Boethius and to many others. She is always *Sapientia creata,* of course; and his poems about her are always *amorous* poems, for he is now truly the *lover* of Sophia. In fact, his praise of her is such that the full range of her meaning requires a very extensive commentary in explication, so extensive that it could not be completed. In any case, these are, and remain, *love* poems, at least the first two of those contemplated for inclusion in the *Convivio.* They celebrate a most ardent *accensio* for this new Lady. The poet is writing in the style of *loda,* yet he has moved quite beyond anything we might recognize as being centrally *within* the cult of courtly love. Now he has set all his heart on *science* and *virtue,* yet he continues in the manner of *amoris accensio.* The first of these *canzoni* addresses the angelic creatures who preside over the third heaven, the heaven of Venus, of course; so that *venus* (but how changed is the meaning!) is very much his theme. Beatrice, moreover, Beatrice *in gloria* (with whom he begins the *Vita Nuova: la gloriosa donna de la mia mente*) is remembered in this first *canzone,* as also in the prose that introduces it. We can remain puzzled as to just how we are to understand that the compassionate lady of the earlier work was *really* this Lady Philosophy who is being celebrated now (and so the *Convivio* would have it); but the fact remains that Dante tells us this very clearly, and it is simply for us to understand the identification as best we can. Dante, in any case, is determined to have it so, for he could so easily have written about this his new love for Philosophy without ever mentioning the *Vita Nuova*; but no, this second work must be firmly tied into the first. Indeed, this very insistence that there be a *continuity* between the two works is itself so characteristic of Dante that we may say it is almost a "constant" with him. For if we now think of the third and last great work of that famous triad, the *Commedia*, we shall have to recognize that it, the third, displays at the outset its relation to the second, the *Convivio*. I refer to Virgil's words of recognition as addressed to Beatrice in the second Canto, wherein we may not fail to see the precise definition (and in a single terzina) of the Lady of the Convivio:

> O donna di virtù, sola per cui
> l'umana spezie eccede ogni contento
> di quel ciel c'ha minor li cerchi sui.[5]

We are thus obliged to recognize, at once, that the Beatrice of the *Commedia* has so grown in her meaning as to *include* the Lady of the *Convivio*, at the same time remaining the Beatrice of the *Vita Nuova*—as is evident when she comes to him at the top of Mount Purgatory to satisfy his "ten-year thirst." But this line of continuity, these organic connections between the three great works, may not be discussed here in any detail.

Indeed, a paper that clearly threatens to grow too long and perhaps too specialized for my present audience, should now be concluded with our eyes directed upon the two terms in the *De vulgari eloquentia* which I have thought might be meaningful for us as we debate the meaning of courtly love: *amoris accensio* and *directio voluntatis*. Certainly it proves meaningful for the student of Dante to look at his total poetic production through these conceptions, which are of his own phrasing.

Having made his beginning, as poet, in the mode of courtly love (*amoris accensio*) Dante came to feel, possibly by 1307–8, that he was no longer a poet of that kind of love, but instead was now dedicated to the subject of *virtus* or *rectitudo*, that he was a poet concerned with "directing the will," or (shall we say) with the "direction of the will." It does not much matter how we translate the terms, for both noun and verb are implied in *directio*. Moreover, we know very well, without having to have Dante tell us so explicitly (and this he does not do) that he had indeed excelled in the mode of *directio voluntatis* years before he penned the words in the *De vulgari*. What else is the *Vita Nuova* itself if not a work in the style named *directio voluntatis?* Precisely the story that surrounds the poems of the *Vita Nuova* is itself a *directio voluntatis*, for Beatrice becomes the guide of course, the director of her lover's will, of his love and his affections, guiding toward that Good beyond which there is nothing to aspire to. And, in so far as it is possible for the reader of the *Vita Nuova* to "identify" with the poet-narrator, the reader too has his will directed by this miracle named Beatrice. There is no time here (and perhaps little need) to examine these matters in any detail.[6]

Let us rather, in concluding, recall the end of the story of Dante's love for Beatrice, which is in itself the perfect completion of the whole history of *directio voluntatis* through her. When at the end (or almost) Dante is privileged to look up to his *gloriosa donna* where she has taken her seat in the Eternal Rose, in true glory now (the light of glory streaming down from above), and when he has addressed his last words of thanksgiving to her (his last *loda*) Beatrice looks down at him and smiles—then she turns her eyes back to the "Eternal Fountain." And no gesture ever declared more clearly that to Him belongs the glory, that to Him our wills should be directed, that *He* is terminus, and no one else. *Directio voluntatis:* it is just here that the direction of the will which Dante had finally come to consider himself the poet of finds its supreme enactment as a guidance *through amoris accensio*. For this perhaps is the most interesting point for us finally to consider. *Directio voluntatis*, as Dante has represented it, arises right out of *amoris accensio* and, through the figure of Beatrice, out of a love that is properly termed *courtly*. For Beatrice is a creature of courtly love. She would never have existed, as we know her, had there not been a tradition of courtly love: she was a *madonna* among *madonne*, sung in the manner of *amoris accensio,* as that convention had come out of Provence. Without the *Vita Nuova* and the *Divine Comedy* Beatrice could well have remained just such a *madonna.* But with the *Vita Nuova* (which makes its beginning with the courtly tradition, so that it can clearly and explicitly register the manner and degree in which it *leaves* that tradition behind), Beatrice becomes the vehicle, the God-given means, by which the will of the poet is directed to God. And with the *Vita Nuova,* in this sense, Dante becomes the poet of *directio voluntatis* and remains such a poet through the fragmentary *Convivio,* and then, triumphantly and completely, in the *Commedia.* And all the while, up to the time of the *De vulgari eloquentia,* at least, Dante can play, sometimes, at courtly love, with friend Cino or others. But a more serious play (and it too *is* a play) prevails through and around the figure of a Beatrice-Sapientia.

But in all this have we not recognized that this poet of *directio* never ceases to be a poet of *accensio?* What else is Beatrice, for all the meanings she may take on, if not the object of Dante's most *ardent* love? What else finally is the *Commedia* about if not about the *burning* of love? What matters, finally, is the goal and end of our love, the *direction* our love takes. And here is a poet who found the way whereby a love which began as *courtly* could finally attain, face to face, to a Love that moves all things, and this through an *accensio* that can only come from Him, the Eternal Source: that last turning of Beatrice's eyes could not more clearly declare this.

Perhaps I may terminate these considerations, relevant or not as you may find them in the matter of Courtly Love, by suggesting that we can readily borrow from St. Thomas Aquinas a formula that had served him well and that can, *mutatis mutandis,* serve us equally well as we seek to understand Dante's position within *and* beyond Courtly Love.

As we all know, St. Thomas found the way to reconcile an "Aristotelian" *nature* with a Christian *grace,* on the principle that "gratia non tollit naturam, sed perficit". Now I would suggest that we read *directio voluntatis* in place of *gratia* in this formula, and read *amoris accensionem* in place of *naturam.* And if you will allow me this, then I believe we have as neat a formula as could possibly be found for understanding the meaning of Courtly Love to Dante: for he it was who showed us, excelling as he did in the mode of *directio voluntatis* (shall we not grant him this?), that courtly love *can* be perfected beyond itself—without being abolished.

Notes

1. *De Vulgari eloquentia* II, ii, 6–8, the text of the *Società dantesca italiana*. I herewith give the translation of the Temple Classics edition of the Latin works, in the reprint of 1940, J. M. Dent, London, pp. 70–71. "And, in order to make this clear, it must be observed that, as man has been endowed with a threefold life, namely, vegetable, animal, and rational, he journeys along a threefold road; for in so far as he is vegetable he seeks for what is useful, wherein he is of like nature with plants; in so far as he is animal he seeks for that which is pleasurable, wherein he is of like nature with the brutes; in so far as he is rational he seeks for what is right—and in this he stands alone, or is a partaker of the nature of the angels. It is by these three kinds of life that we appear to carry out whatever we do; and because in each one of them some things are greater, some greatest, within the range of their kind, it follows that those which are greatest appear the ones which ought to be treated of supremely, and consequently, in the greatest vernacular.

"But we must discuss what things are greatest; and first in respect of what is useful. Now in this matter, if we carefully consider the object of all those who are in search of what is useful, we shall find that it is nothing else but safety. Secondly, in respect of what is pleasurable; and here we say that that is most pleasurable which gives pleasure by the most exquisite object of appetite, and this is love. Thirdly, in respect of what is right; and here no one doubts that virtue has the first place. Wherefore these three things, namely, safety, love, and virtue, appear to be those capital matters which ought to be treated of supremely, I mean the things which are most important in respect of them, as prowess in arms, the fire of love, and the direction of the will."

2. I have before me the paperback edition of the Beacon Press, Boston, 1955: J. Huizinga, *Homo ludens: A study of the play-element in culture.*

3. I am glad to be able to refer all readers of Dante's lyrics, and particularly readers who need help with the Italian, to the excellent edition, just out, of *Dante's Lyric Poetry*, by Foster and Boyde, Clarendon Press, in two volumes, Italian text and English prose translation in the first, and an extensive commentary in the second. The correspondence with Cino referred to will be found toward the end of Volume I. The so-called *canzone montanina*, Dante's 'prize-poem' has the *capoverso: Doglia mi reca ne lo core ardire.*

4. *Par.* XX, 121.

5. *Inf.* II, 76–78. On which see C. S. Singleton, *Journey to Beatrice*, Dante Studies 2, Harvard Press, 1958, pp. 127 ff.

6. I may refer the reader, for the detailed analysis, to my *Essay on the Vita Nuova*, Harvard Press, 2nd edition, 1958.

Faith Unfaithful—The German Reaction to Courtly Love

W. T. H. JACKSON
Columbia University

The literature of Germany in the High Middle Ages is largely a reaction to contemporary literature in France. Some French critics—Jeanroy is a good example—prefer to regard it as a mere continuation, an imitation or adaptation of French literature, but this is not so. It is a reaction, sometimes little more than a feeble reworking but more often an attempt to express the thought and style of French literature in new terms. It must be borne in mind that the reaction was to French literature as the German poets understood it, and this understanding was sometimes faulty. Just as for an understanding of classicism it is important to know what an eighteenth-century European believed the Greeks to be, rather than what they actually were, so we must recognize that many German authors failed to perceive the ironical overtones in French literature and reacted to a system of values which they believed to be there. It is interesting that many of their more recent countrymen have done the same.

There is little point in reviving the controversy started by Ehrismann in 1919[1] and continued by Curtius[2] and Neumann,[3] except to point out that they all assume some consistency of attitude in the German authors they are discussing. Most people would agree with Curtius that there is little evidence to link Aristotle with an assumed moral philosophy which is present in the "courtly code." Yet it must be remarked that even Curtius seems to believe that there was such a code, even if it was not formal or written. Ehrismann had advanced the thesis that the German authors derived their code from Wernher von Elmendorf, that is, from philosophical rather than literary sources. The implication would seem to be that the Germans observed a code largely independent of that supposedly derived from the French works they used as models—a scarcely tenable thesis.

There can be little doubt that the German authors saw in the French works they read evidence of a code of ideal behavior for a secular knight. Hartmann von Aue makes it clear that he knows of such a code when he describes, in *Der arme Heinrich*, the man who has every virtue to give him social grace and distinction but lacks humility and charity.[4]

We are fortunate to be able to make direct comparisons between many major German narrative works and their French originals—the two romances of Hartmann von Aue and Wolfram's *Parzival* are based directly on the works of Chrétien de Troyes, even if additional material is used by both authors, and Gottfried von Strassburg acknowledges Thomas of Britain as his model. Konrad von Würzburg and Rudolf von Ems make extensive use of extant French works. In lyric poetry there is no acknowledgement by the Germans but a great deal of obvious borrowing, both of style and content. We might expect, therefore, that the German works would follow their French models closely in their depicting of the love phenomenon. Yet quite the opposite is the case. Each author chose works which suited his purpose and modified the treatment of love which he found there.

It is not surprising that Hartmann should have chosen the *Erec* and the *Yvain*. The two works, particularly *Yvain*, seem to present a neat formulation of the love-adventure problem, so neat, in fact, that the literary histories have found them complementary, two works showing adventure neglected for love and love neglected for adventure. The formulation is too simple, for Chrétien does not present love in *Erec* as he does in *Yvain*. Enide is a simple, unsophisticated girl who is unaffected by courtly trappings, while Laudine is a widow whose moves are calculated in accordance with her social position. If we are to assume that it is characteristic of courtly love that the lady be won by unremitting service, then neither *Erec* nor *Yvain* shows evidence of the phenomenon. Enide is won by the usual method employed by medieval suitors who were not in Arthurian romances. Erec says that he would like to take her to the tournament where he intends to compete for the prize of the sparrow-hawk; if her father agrees, Erec will return the favor by marrying her. It is a business arrangement. Erec never says at this stage that he loves Enide, nor does he ask whether she cares for him; nevertheless, Enide is "honored" to accept the proposition. After all, she is living in fairly straitened circumstances with her father but if she marries Erec, she will be a queen. Chrétien is careful to point out the difference between the unspoilt Enide and the artificial and calculating ladies of Guenevere's court. Enide's reaction to the rumors about Erec's idleness and its effect on his men is therefore entirely natural. She does not want her husband to look bad in the eyes of his peers. Guenevere does not care how bad Lancelot looks, so long as she can demonstrate her power over him. Erec appreciates Enide's love when he hears her reject the overtures of the Count of Limors under circumstances which could not possibly be feigned. But even after this experience he does not perform love-service for her. He serves a greater cause and she is his champion. The concluding "Joie de la Cort" episode makes very clear the difference between the servile bondage of a knight to a lady's whim and the free association of lovers in a purposeful life. The association of Erec and Enide begins without sighs or complaints and it ends in a loving companionship. By no stretch of imagination can the term "courtly" be applied to it, except in the very limited sense that Enide is a noble creature who inspires Erec.

Hartmann von Aue has even less to say about the early meetings of Erec and Enide than Chrétien has. In his version Enide does not even say that she will be honored to accept. It is clear that Chrétien and Hartmann following him were thinking in terms of *mutual* love between the sexes. As Furstner has pointed out,[5] such mutuality is not a characteristic of many so-called courtly works, least of all of the love found in lyric poetry. That love is rather admiration of specific qualities in the lady, qualities which are carefully enumerated and described. It is this assessment of qualities rather than love for the lady as a person which brings about the effect commented on by so many critics: that the lover does not appear to be in love with a lady at all or, if he is, it is with the same lady who has been eulogized by many other lyric poets. In the last analysis such love consists in the recognition of the presence of abstract qualities and does not call for any corresponding recognition from the lady. It is not love but worship.

Yvain's love, on the other hand, is of the courtly order. Chrétien makes this clear by several stylistic devices. The first is the use of the internal monologue, which shows the hero analyzing the reasons why he loves and weighing the obstacles to that love in pseudo-rational fashion. Another device is the personification of love as a power which exercises dominance in the most unlikely situations, which wounds and cures the wounds it makes. There are also the required fervid descriptions but here they are ironical, leading as they do to the interview with Laudine in which Yvain's protestations of eternal fidelity and complete subservience to his lady cause him to be employed as defender of the fountain. Laudine does not say that she loves him at this point; the relation is one of service. Only when she permits him to go on adventure does she show any signs of affection by giving him a ring which will prevent him from being wounded. When he is received back, she again fails to show any signs of affection. On the contrary, she says that she has been deceived into taking him back and that only the oath she has sworn forces her to accept him. All she allows is peace between them. Chrétien's version of the Yvain story demonstrates with full irony the difference between service and love.

The irony is not so clear in the version of Hartmann von Aue. He follows Chrétien closely, even to the point of literal translation of some passages, but he expands the scenes in which Iwein's love is depicted and he dilates more than does Chrétien on the power of love. It is in the final scene, however, that Hartmann proves that he has misunderstood his source. Quite gratuitously he adds to Chrétien's ironical conclusion a scene in which Laudine falls at Iwein's feet and begs his forgiveness for all the trouble she has caused him.[6] The action is utterly out of character. It is Iwein who raises Laudine to her feet and is all magnanimity. Hartmann has achieved his happy ending and made love conquer all, but he has misunderstood Chrétien's purpose. Clearly Hartmann believed that there was such a thing as courtly love and that it brought lovers together into harmony. In appreciating each other's virtues, they loved. The thought is touching, but it was not what Chrétien believed nor, as we shall see, did Hartmann's great German contemporaries follow him.

Wolfram von Eschenbach denies that he owes anything to the *Conte del Graal* of Chrétien de Troyes, although he mentions Chrétien's name in a manner which makes it seem likely that he would expect his audience to assume that he had used the French author as a source. It is, in fact, perfectly clear from a comparison of *Parzival* and the *Conte del Graal* that Wolfram has taken much of his material from the French poem but has modified it wherever he felt that it failed to express his views or where, more important, he felt that views were advanced, particularly about women, which conflicted sharply with his own. It is almost impossible to say what Chrétien intended to do with his heroine Blanscheflur. She appears only in one scene and that a very conventional one. She is the lady besieged—by potential lovers whom she dislikes, and Perceval arrives in the nick of time to rescue her. Presumably it is feminine intuition which tells her that the newly-arrived Red Knight can save her from her enemies, for she goes to great lengths to win him to her. The situation is not precisely one in which the knight volunteers his services. He is in his room, retired for the night, when she comes to him and exerts her charms to win him to her side. Perceval may be a boor, crude and unpolished, but innocent he is not. Even at the earliest stage of his knightly career he was able to appreciate the difference between the kisses he forced from the lady in the tent and those of his mother's serving maids. There can be little doubt that Perceval enjoyed his night with Blanscheflur and that not allegorically. How courtly can such a situation be? If aloofness is the mark, we do not have it here. Nor is there any love-service, only the promise of practical support. Further relations between the two are on a sensual level. After Perceval leaves Blanscheflur he remembers her, so far as we are informed, only on the occasion of his seeing the blood in the snow. She plays no further part in his progress. The situation is quite different in Wolfram's poem, as we shall see.

Wolfram frequently addresses his audience in the first person, but by far the most important instance of such communication is that which, significantly, appears between the second and third books of *Parzival*. Wolfram has just completed the introduction to his poem, an introduction which owes nothing to Chrétien or indeed to any known work, and is about to embark on his main theme, which, as he was well aware, followed Chrétien's poem very closely. Here was the point at which he should make his intentions clear. He might be following the story, but he was not following the morality. And in particular he wished to make it perfectly clear that he did not accept the attitude toward women which he found in earlier works. His statements on the subject are worth analyzing. He claims that he has nothing against women and is glad to hear their praises, but one woman has aroused his ire and with her he can never be reconciled. He accuses her of unfaithfulness and states that she has enlisted the support of other women against him. There is no clear indication of the identity of this woman, and earlier commentators thought of her as an actual person who had proved unfaithful to the poet. More recently scholars have tended to believe that the lady referred to is Isolde and that the whole passage is a reference to the continuing and fundamental disagreement between Wolfram and Gottfried von Strassburg.[7] This is very probably true, but it does not alter the much more fundamental point that Wolfram is opposed not to Isolde alone but to the feminine society which, in his opinion, she represents. His reference to the large number of women makes this clear. He also leaves no doubt of the characteristic which makes him despise them—*untriuwe*, faithlessness. It may seem strange that he should single out this quality when the courtly writers themselves emphasize that faithfulness in love is highly desirable. The difference lies in the object of that faithfulness. Isolde was faithful to Tristan but that does not absolve her from guilt in Wolfram's eyes; for him there is only one kind of faithfulness, that between husband and wife. Wolfram makes this last point abundantly clear by his careful gradation of women. It is not hard to show parallels between the most important women of the Parzival story and those of the Gawan adventures. One or two of the female characters appear in both parts with different characteristics. Parzival meets Sigune much earlier in the work than Perceval meets his unnamed cousin, and it seems likely that this was an intentional change on Wolfram's part, for Sigune and Jeschute are clearly contrasted. Schionatulander, Sigune's lover, is killed by Orilus because of Sigune's absurd demand that he demonstrate his

Minnedienst by undertaking adventure in her name. It is the same Orilus who is capable of believing that Jeschute is unfaithful to him. His brutal treatment of her is ended only by his defeat at the hands of Parzival, a defeat, incidentally, which fulfills his unthinking promise to avenge Sigune when she first tells him of her loss. Thus both Sigune and Jeschute have lost their lovers, the latter through a blunder by a boy who thought himself courtly and through the vulgarity of a man who was professedly a courtly lover, the former through a mistaken belief in "adventure." It is courtliness which is responsible for both tragedies. Both these incidents appear in Chrétien's work, but the treatment is different. In the "Lady in the Tent" scene, Chrétien's emphasis is entirely on the blunders of Perceval. Wolfram emphasizes the luscious beauty of the lady and in doing so is careful to make clear that his hero is untouched by it. There can be no reference to the sweetness of the lady's kisses. Later, when Jeschute is being driven in rags through the forest, Wolfram has plenty of time to dwell upon those charming parts of her body whose well-turned beauty cannot be hidden by her inadequate clothing. Her reconciliation with Orilus is described entirely in physical terms and it is brought about by physical methods. Quite the opposite is true of Sigune. As the story progresses, her concern for the affairs of this world grows less and less. Her spiritual progress is actually in advance of that of Parzival. She assures herself that Schionatulander was actually her husband, even though they were never officially married. It is, of course, impossible to tell what Chétien would have made of the character of Perceval's cousin if he had completed his romance. There is little evidence, however, that he had any intention of depicting the spiritualized figure who appears in Wolfram's work. Both Jeschute and Sigune show the disastrous effects of an aspect of courtly love which Wolfram mentions in the remarks to which we have already referred—the desire on the part of the knight to demonstrate that only one lady, his own beloved, can be considered "fair." Wolfram makes a mockery of the suggestion by showing what happened to two very different ladies whose lovers practiced such a creed.

The picture of the demanding lady is made even more absurd by the contrast between Orgeluse and Condwiramurs. We should note that Orgeluse has a part in both the Parzival story and the

Gawan adventures. It is she who has caused Amfortas to lose his kingship by his pursuit of unchaste love. She fails to persuade Parzival to follow the same path. Her relations with Gawan are almost a parody of the *Minnedienst* situation. She orders him to perform deeds which are obviously designed to bring about his death, so that service to her is virtually fatal, and any other knight but Gawan (or, of course, Parzival) must inevitably have perished. And all this is accompanied by scorn and disgust. Surely, one would say, we have here a parody of the courtly lady, a Guenevere on an even lower plane, who tests her knight not by making him lose tournaments but by sending him to his death. Yet she has her reasons. Like Sigune, she has lost her lover in the courtly game, lost him to a man who, like Orilus, is not a murderer but an unthinking participant in a system which demanded that men kill or be killed in defense of their lady's fame—not her honor in any moral sense. Sigune lost Schionatulander in this way and Orgeluse lost Zidegast. Her fatal influence impinged upon the Grail story in her luring of Amfortas from his dedication to the pure love of the Grail. Thus her conduct towards Gawan takes on an altogether different aspect. She was avenging herself, not on Gawan himself, but on a system which had deprived her of her lover and she was doing so by pushing that system to its logical end—by insisting that as a potential lover he should undertake tasks entirely because she told him to do so, without promise of reward and entirely as a matter of service. It is only when he does these things without flinching and meets with Gramoflanz, her lover's killer, that she breaks down and confesses her reasons.

Now all these events are to be found in the version of Chrétien de Troyes, and I have little doubt that he intended to make an ironic commentary on the courtly system. He does so in all his works. But because his poem is unfinished we cannot tell whether he intended the contrast which Wolfram makes so pointedly. Sigune's reaction to the death of her lover is to turn to the spiritual life. It is a personal devotion rather than participation in the spiritual fellowship of the Grail company, but it is clearly oriented to religion, as can be seen in her successive appearances—first as a fresh girl, emaciated and sad after Parzival has left the Grail castle, then in a hermit's cell as Parzival approaches Trevrizent for the discussion which is the turning point of his career, and finally dead in her cell as Parzival makes his way again to the Grail castle. She rejects the secular for the spiritual, but there is no evidence that her nameless counterpart in Chrétien's work would have done the same. Chrétien's lady sorrows over her dead lover, but far from taking refuge in the spiritual, wishes that her lover's killer could himself be killed. The explanation for the difference between the two works lies in the fact that Chrétien does not envisage a separate, spiritually oriented Grail community as an alternative to a secularly oriented Arthurian world. His criticism of that world remains, in his extant work, criticism and no positive alternative is offered.

Wolfram's criticism of the idea of love-service is quite explicit. He has no time for the kind of man who overpraises his lady and regards her as the only one worthy of consideration. He does not consider that it is a knight's duty to maintain such a belief, nor should the lady expect it. If she wants him, she should do so on the basis of his knightly conduct in general rather than his service to her in particular. Thus Wolfram clearly states that service to the lady is not the most important part of knightly duty and that knightly combat is not intended for the winning of ladies but for higher objectives. Gawan may spend his time in this fashion but, as we have seen, Gawan is on a much lower level than Parzival— and even he marries his lady before winning her love. It is not too much to say that all knights who are obsessed with the idea of love-service prove defective in one way or another—Orilus is a fine example—until they bow to circumstances and marry their ladies. But Parzival goes much further. His service to women is of a very different order. At no point does he set out to win any woman's love by service. He does reject Orgeluse, whom Gawan serves. His wife comes to him for help and that help is granted, not out of any belief that it would win her love, but because she is a helpless creature opposed by overwhelming forces. Wolfram goes to great lengths to emphasize the unimportance of *Minne* in their relationship. He changes even small details of Chrétien's narrative of the visit of Blanscheflur to Perceval in order to stress the chastity of the meeting of his own characters. He is careful to have them married, as Chrétien's lovers are not, and even after they are married, he shows them postponing the consummation of the marriage for three days. Wolfram has no patience with love as a mere expression of physical desire, as he tells us in his own person, and he has even less with those women who use their charms to allure men to do their bidding. In this respect he is closer to the attitude of the Church than he is to that of the romance.

Parzival leaves his wife in order to search for his mother. He does not see Condwiramurs again until his second visit to the Grail castle. The only occasion on which there is any lengthy reference to her before this is when he is fascinated by the drops of blood in the snow and is reminded of the beauty of his beloved. Hers is an abstract, magical beauty whose form is close to the conventional imagery applied to the Virgin. Although he found the incident in his source, Wolfram had no objection to it since it did not represent any physical appearance by Condwiramurs during the period of Parzival's trial. For Parzival's struggle for the Grail kingdom concentrates on that alone, and this concentration constitutes the sharpest contrast between his behavior and that of Gawan. Gawan's fight is for love. All the combats in which he engages after his first meeting with Orgeluse are directly or indirectly designed to further his attempt to win her. Knightly adventure is, for him, subordinated to the pursuit of love, the very point which Wolfram attacks so sharply in the prologue to Book III and which, incidentally, he was to make the main aim of the pagan, as contrasted to the Christian, pursuit of religion in his other major narrative poem, *Willehalm*.

Wolfram makes very clear what he believes to be the function of the female in knightly endeavor. Condwiramurs meets Parzival again when he attains the Grail castle for the second time—and she brings with her two children. Her marriage has already assured Parzival that he will have not only a son to succeed him but another who can carry out the other major function of the Grail knights, the aiding of distressed persons, particularly rulers. The stress on the family and its continuation is as evident here as it is throughout Wolfram's work. But the women have another function. They, not the men, are the true guardians of the sacred vessel. It is kept in the women's quarters and attended entirely by them. Parzival is connected with the Grail through Herzeloyde, his mother, and it is clear that Wolfram considers that the spiritual qualities are to be sought in the female rather than in the male. Yet his Grail guardians are far from being Vestal Virgins. They can and do marry and leave the Grail castle, but their offspring return to the service of the Grail.

No better example of Wolfram's attitude towards *Minnedienst* could be chosen than the story of Parzival's brother Feirefis. When he encounters Parzival he is indeed seeking his father but he is also maintaining the supremacy of his lady, Sekundille, queen of "India," to whom he is married. Thus, although he has never been to Arthur's court or, so far as we know, been instructed in the niceties of courtly love, he is following the standard and, in Wolfram's view, ridiculous, practice of seeking adventure to prove his love. All this obsession fades as soon as he sees Repanse de Schoye, the chief guardian of the Grail, who is Parzival's aunt and quite literally old enough to be Feirefis' mother. But the Grail has kept her young. All thoughts of Sekundille disappear in a flash. He desires Repanse de Schoye alone and he attains her by being baptized a Christian. Wolfram makes no secret of the fact that it is to win a lady that Feirefis is baptized, but for Wolfram there exists no essential difference between Christian and pagan except the fact of baptism. By the act of becoming a Christian, Feirefis abandons love-service in the courtly sense; he exchanges a lower for a higher form both in religion and in love.

Thus Wolfram makes clear his criticism of the ideas of love which he had received from his sources. He rejects the two basic constituents of courtly love, the right of a woman to demand unquestioning service in whatever triviality she fancies, and the need for a knight to gain honor for his lady by embarking on a series of otherwise pointless adventures, adventures which often result in the death of innocent persons and lifelong grief to others with whom the knight has no personal quarrel, nor even grounds for quarreling. We have already noted than Chrétien is critical of courtly love, but his criticism takes the form of ironical comment, not of fundamental rejection. The fact is that Wolfram is writing for life. He emphasizes the didactic sense of his work and its application to the conduct of his audience. Yet he is reacting to a literary courtly ideal which he must have recognized in the works he had read and which, unless he crassly misunderstood his source, as I sometimes suspect, he did not find in the works of Chrétien de Troyes. Wolfram, in other words, saw in the current ideals of love-service a clear danger to his own standards of morals.

Wolfram von Eschenbach and Gottfried von Strassburg found little on which they could agree and indeed went out of their way to make unobliging remarks about each other. But on one thing they were in complete accord—they both disliked the ideas of courtly love which they found in current literature. So far as our knowledge goes, there could have been very little written in German at this time to call forth their ire. Only Hartmann von Aue, Heinrich von Veldeke, and perhaps Ulrich von Zazikhoven had written anything of any significance and both Wolfram and Gottfried are loud in their praise of Hartmann. They must have been reacting principally to the French literature of their day. Gottfried's reasons for disliking courtly literature are quite different from those of Wolfram and he is even more explicit about them.

Gottfried's approach is intellectual rather than moral or social. He is concerned with love as a phenomenon, not as something which may affect contemporary life for good or evil. In fact, it becomes very clear in his work that he is perfectly well aware of the enormous potentiality for evil which love may have. Gottfried sets forth his thesis in the prologue to his *Tristan*, and although the language is deliberately ambivalent, the thesis itself is clear. Most authors regard love as one of the world's pleasures. They are concerned with it only as an element in the leisure time of a knight. Their purpose is to describe only the joys of love, not its full nature. Gottfried says that he has no objection to these people, since they are doing their best but he asks indulgence if he decides to take a different point of view. That point of view will be that there is no certainty in love, that its nature is shifting and imprecise, affecting different people in different ways but showing one characteristic in all cases—its immense power. It should be noted at once that we are not discussing here whether love is sensual or spiritual, whether it is *amor purus* or *amor mixtus*. Gottfried assumes that there will be a sensual element in all love. Otherwise it would not exist. His interest lies rather in the relation of love to the totality of existence. In earlier works in which love at court had been shown, the situation was fairly simple. The love of a woman was sought by a knight. His service to her might take the form of defending her honor, of winning tournaments in her name, of maintaining her beauty and other qualities before all comers, even, in the lyrics, of praising her in verse. These are his services to her. They show the knight's love as a form of homage, a homage for which he should receive his reward. In the romances he does receive that reward, and it is certainly not true that in narrative poetry courtly love means unrequited love. The *canso* has as a convention that the lady is beyond the lover's reach, but the convention does not apply to the romances. Gottfried never concerns himself with this "unattainability" convention, since love cannot exist if it is not mutual. He is concerned, however, with the service-reward relationship and with the reasons why people fall in love.

Curious as it may seem, French narrative poetry gives little attention to the reasons why people love. In *Cligès* and *Yvain* we are shown the deadly effects of the sight of the beloved upon the knight and in *Cligès*—but not in *Yvain*—of the knight on the lady. The process of falling in love is brought about by sight, by the image, but further details are usually lacking. Again there is none of the analysis we find in lyric poetry, especially in later Italian. The interest of the love story lies in the later justification of the love through adventure and service. In *Lancelot, Erec,* and *Perceval* there is not even a preliminary description of the devastating effects of the lady's eyes. Lancelot is already in love at the opening of the poem, Erec wins his bride originally because he needs her for adventure, and Perceval (in the French version) enjoys his love as part of the defense of his lady's lands. Falling in love is an abstraction leading to homage through adventure. The lover thinks that his lady is the most beautiful and virtuous lady in the world—but what lover does not? We are never told precisely what it is that makes lovers attractive to one another.

Gottfried takes a very different view of the problem. He is concerned that his readers should know what steps lead to love on the various levels at which it may be conceived. Hence his work begins not with the story of Tristan but with that of his father, Riwalin. Blanscheflur, the sister of king Mark, is attracted to Riwalin when she sees him riding at Tintagel and later in a tournament. This attraction is conventional, brought about by the eyes, a fact which Gottfried emphasizes by the nature of his descriptions. Here we have the clichés of courtly love, and they are reinforced by the description of the perfect May weather of the tournament, the ideal landscape, and the glory of the court. When Riwalin is gravely wounded in battle, there is much neat play on the wound of love-cure of love topos, but oddly enough, when Riwalin recovers, he is quite prepared to terminate the affair with suitable protestations of sorrow. The situation is that of the *Aeneid*, with one important difference. Blanscheflur is expecting a child, and at this disclosure Riwalin's honor is affected. He cannot leave Blanscheflur to be publicly disgraced, since his own honor would be impugned, and he therefore offers to take her with him. Later the two are married and Tristan, at least according to the law in some countries, was born legitimate. It will be noticed that the child is the only reason for Riwalin's taking of Blanscheflur with him. Otherwise this "typical" courtly romance would have come to an abrupt end. As the flowers of May fade, so does love. There is no basis for love here except physical attraction expressed in visual terms. Nor is there any thought of permanence. Gottfried shows us that Tristan's birth is the result of a union whose aim was pure joy, and that the partners in the liaison had no thought of love beyond self-gratification. Sorrow was indeed present, because Riwalin was wounded in the tournament, but sorrow was not an essential part of their love.

The description of the *enfance* of the hero is common enough in the romances, but Gottfried's description of Tristan's education goes far beyond the normal. It concentrates on the aesthetic attainments, on the development of a cultured personality, and dwells on two aspects of Tristan's training in particular, his skill in languages and his power in music. I use the word "power" advisedly, for Tristan does not merely possess a high degree of performing skills. He is technically accomplished and thereby gains admiration, but his music wins over men to such a degree that they have no power over themselves and are no longer capable of rational thought. They can do nothing but respond to the music he plays. Gottfried makes this clear on several occasions, but the most important by far is Tristan's use of music to gain entrance to the court of Ireland. The common people are drawn by the charm of his music, Isolde's tutor by its great technical skill. It is this music which brings him to Isolde.

It is worth examining the description of their first meeting with some care: "And so they sent for his harp and the young Princess, too, was summoned. Lovely Isolde, Love's true signet, with which in days to come his heart was sealed and locked from all the world save her alone, Isolde also repaired there and attended closely to Tristan as he sat and played his harp. And indeed, now that he had hopes that his misfortunes were over, he was playing better than had ever played before, for he to them played not as a lifeless man; he went to work with animation, like one in the best of spirits."[8] There are several noteworthy points about this meeting. The first is that Tristan does not react to Isolde's presence at all, nor does she to his. He sees her as any lover in the romances sees his lady, but there is no overwhelming impact, no love at first sight. The most enduring love affair in medieval literature begins with no sign of affection on either side. But there is a second and perhaps more significant aspect. We have noted the stress on the visual in falling in love, courtly fashion. Herbert Kolb, in his monumental work *Der Begriff der Minne*, rightly devotes a long chapter to the discussion of "Die Mystik des Auges und des Herzens,"[9] for in all lyric poetry from Guillaume de Poitiers to Petrarch, love is a matter of sight. Not so in Gottfried's poem. Tristan himself says that he will be cured "through his music," and it is through music that he moves to love. In the highly detailed description that Gottfried offers of the instruction of Isolde, the stress is always on sound—on language and on music. It is through them that she learns, as Tristan had, to move the hearts of men and render them incapable of rational thinking. The "moraliteit" which he teaches her is, as I have pointed out elsewhere,[10] closely connected with music, with the forming of character by musical means. Isolde moves on the same level as Tristan, she is prepared for a kind of love different from that found in the earlier romances and, let us observe, different from that of Riwalin and Blanscheflur, whose attraction was visual and physical.

Although the practice of music establishes a kind of harmony between Tristan and Isolde which is to be found between no other characters in the poem, it does not make them fall in love. The most diligent search fails to reveal any indication of love at this stage. Tristan is, after all, Tantris and hence not noble, so far as the Irish court knows. The invention of a wife as an excuse for leaving is an ironical comment on courtly love. The irony becomes more marked when Tristan returns to Ireland to woo Isolde for Mark. He knows that Isolde can be won by an act of service—killing the dragon—and Gottfried stresses this fact. The whole incident in Ireland is a mockery of the service-reward cliché of courtly love. Tristan kills the dragon, cuts out its tongue and is promptly rewarded for his pains by being poisoned. The reason is, of course, that he cannot go around with a dragon's head in his hand, and his plans are uncertain because he cannot declare himself as Mark's envoy. He is, to use an expression appropriate to Tristan, playing it by ear. The seneschal who cuts off the dragon's head has no such problems. To him the equation is simple: a seneschal (inevitably of noble birth) plus one dragon's head equals a suitor for the hand of Isolde. There would be nothing remarkable about this if he had really killed the dragon. Courtly romance is full of such incidents. Isolde despises the seneschal, and the thought of marrying him disgusts her, but she and her mother realize that there is no escape unless it can be proved that he is a liar. Tristan saves Isolde when he is able to show that it was he who performed the service. In the version of Thomas of Britain, Tristan uses this very point to stop Isolde from killing him in the bath—"kill me and you will have to marry the seneschal"—but for Gottfried this was too crass. His hero appeals to Isolde's honor. As a lady, she cannot kill a defenseless man. All this should not blind us to the fact that no one disputes the seneschal's right to marry Isolde. Love or no love, he has performed his service and is entitled to his reward. And dragon-slaying was definitely a recognized form of service. Nor should we fail to notice that Isolde is to marry Mark for the same reason—Tristan has performed the service of killing the dragon and now has the right to dispose of Isolde's person. He could marry her himself, but his loyalty to Mark causes him to delegate his rights to his sovereign. No wonder Isolde complains. She has escaped the seneschal only to be handed over to a foreign king whom she has never seen. "You have won me by guile from those who brought me up, and are taking me I know not where! I have no idea what fate I have been sold into, nor what is going to become of me!"[11] Tristan's reply is to offer her social advantages, and she is unmoved. Yet Tristan's actions have in fact followed the rules of courtly love—he has performed the right actions to win his lady, but he has not won her for himself. It is Mark who will enjoy the fruit of his *Minnedienst* and that fruit will be his purely sensual enjoyment of Isolde. This is something less than true love, particularly since Mark's first experience with his "wife" is really with Brangaene, and Mark is utterly unable to distinguish between the two.

Tristan and Isolde come to love each other on the ship. There are no special circumstances which bring about their love except that the close conditions on shipboard throw them together. The ground has long been prepared, and Isolde has already given evidence that she is in love with Tristan, although the reverse cannot be said to be true. If the love-potion means anything, it is that a wave of conscious physical attraction sweeps over them both. They are aware of love and, each for different reasons, struggle against it. Love does indeed conquer all but not in the trite fashion of conventional romance. It is an overmastering desire which is far removed from the self-conscious agonies of Alexander in *Cligès*, from the sensual daydreams of Lavinia and Aeneas, from the maunderings of Yvain at his first sight of Laudine. It is, perhaps, closest to the feelings of Lancelot but with the important difference that the idea of making Tristan serve her as Lancelot serves Guenevere never enters Isolde's head. Quite the contrary. When he is in exile and wins for her a little dog, Petitcriu, whose bell will delight her with its music, she tears the bell from its neck so that she will not have pleasure while Tristan suffers pain.

Each of the lovers has only one thought—to be with the other. Neither considers that there is any obligation of service between them. Yet it is perhaps inevitable that the early stages of their love should follow a pattern of courtly intrigue and that Brangaene in a positive sense and Melot in a negative sense should regard their love affair in this light. Other authors, Eilhart and the authors of the prose versions, do in fact so regard it. Only very slowly do the lovers themselves come to realize what "Tristan-love" involves, and it is something very different from courtly love. The scene in the grotto of love is the key to Gottfried's *Tristan*, as the scene in the hermit's cave is to *Parzival*. It is distinguished by several important features. The first is the separation of the grotto from civilized life. It is utterly cut off from the court by mountains and dense woods. The grotto itself is set in a *paysage idéal*, strongly reminiscent of, but by no means identical with, the landscape of Mark's court at the meeting of Riwalin and Blanscheflur. Secondly, it is pagan. The cave is specifically said to date from pre-Christian times and to have been made in honor of the pagan goddess of love. Yet the symbolism used is similar to the conventional allegorization of the Christian church building in terms of the *Ecclesia Dei*. Thus it is at once a temple for the worship of love and a shrine within the heart of every lover in which love can dwell. Perhaps most important of all is the fact that the lovers are alone there. Their life is concentrated entirely on love, which means on each other. Moreover their love is mutual in the sense that neither is regarded as the active or passive partner. Gottfried emphasizes this mutuality by his description of their playing instruments and singing, each in turn taking the part of instrumentalist and vocalist. Such a scene is unparalleled in works which profess to treat of courtly love or are presumed to do so. When Erec devotes himself entirely to his wife, he is accused of uxoriousness, of neglecting his knightly duty, and the remainder of the romance is devoted to his rehabilitation. In other words, courtly love is a social matter. Whatever our view of the existence of a courtly code, of a type of love called courtly, there is no denying that the French romances and many of their German imitators see love as part of a system of social behavior. It bestows dignity and honor on a man, it gives respect to a woman. Without it both knight and lady are incomplete members of society. Further, it influences the knight's total behavior, his use of prowess, and the kind of adventure on which he embarks. All these aspects of love in the romances are denied by Gottfried's *Tristan*. Love is entirely individual; it exists between lovers only. The opinion of other members of society is immaterial and should be considered only in so far as flouting it may create difficulties for the lovers. Adventure is not made more purposeful by the fact that love inspires it. Bluntly, courtly society is inimical to true love. Many members of that society are of too base a clay to be able to appreciate it—Melot and the seneschals are good examples—but even those who, as persons, are noble and kind, such as Mark and Brangaene, are unable to understand. Gottfried's poem raises the fundamental question about true love—is it, in fact, compatible with society at all? If Gottfried's poem had been completed we should presumably have his answer. As it is, we can say only that it appears that either society or love must break in the struggle and that it would have been the lovers who were crushed.

Gottfried thus denies the essentially comic (in the medieval sense) outcome of love at court. The happy ending which comes from the individual's learning to adjust to the needs of courtly society and from the modification of courtly attitudes because of the hero's achievements is impossible in his story. Love is fundamentally incompatible with courtly life. There is, in fact, no such thing as courtly love, for such an expression would be a contradiction in terms. The court is an artificial organization which is conducted by a series of shams. Gottfried says in his prologue and continues to say throughout the poem that there are many decent and well-meaning people in courtly society and that they should be honored as such. But the system, represented by the seneschals and their like, restricts even the good.

We should at this point note one essential difference between Wolfram and Gottfried. Wolfram did not regard himself as primarily a writer. He thought of himself as a knight. His remarks on love may be taken to express his personal beliefs and to be didactic in the sense that contemporaries could follow them in their daily lives. This is not Gottfried's sense of his own mission. He is an artist who is examining the phenomenon of love, of noble love. Inevitably, his milieu is that of the court—no other would have been conceivable in his day—but he is not didactic. His characters are exemplary, they are martyrs of love but they belong to the literary and artistic world.

The histories of German literature often divide later German writers of romance into the successors of Wolfram and the successors of Gottfried. In fact they had no successors. Whatever superficial resemblances of style or treatment are to be found, the later writers did not treat love in the same way as either of these two authors. Even the continuators of Gottfried were unable to finish his poem in the sense in which he had written. Konrad von Würzburg, Rudolf von Ems and their like sentimentalize love, and this is the fate we would expect of a system whose principal constituent was slavish devotion.

The German reaction to love in French and Provençal lyric poetry is really a different subject from that we have been discussing. One of the great disadvantages of a term like "courtly love" is the ease with which it can be stretched to cover many different types and genres. The German love lyric is courtly only in the sense that the men who wrote it were at least technically noblemen who had connections at court. At the end of the twelfth century the only alternative to this would have been that they should be clerics. For the early imitators of Provençal and French poetry, love is indeed ennobling but there is no theoretical reason, implied or stated, that only those of noble birth can participate in it. Heinrich von Morungen feels as strongly as Guido Guinizelli that it is the noble heart that loves a noble lady and that it is character not birth which decides nobility. Those elements in Provençal poetry which might conceivably be called courtly, particularly the formal panegyric of an actual lady, even though she be concealed under a *senhal*, are conspicuously absent. Even when reference is made to a specific lady, the interest is concentrated on the love felt by the poet. It is not too much to speak of the persona of the lady and the persona of the poet set in a situation of tension with each other. Yet it cannot be denied that the essential element of courtly love, *Minnedienst* or love-service, is stressed by all the poets before Walther von der Vogelweide and many after. In the work of Heinrich von Morungen, the relation is expressed by a series of images, though not without ironical overtones, while Reinmar von Hagenau anticipates the *dolce stil nuovo* in his rational language and analytical approach. Yet in both there is an absence of metaphysical concepts. The analysis is of the feelings, the emotions, the reasons for continuing to serve a lady with song, even though any reward seems remote.

The approach was sterile. In a few years all its possibilities had been exhausted. No amount of discussion could provide a reason for a love relationship which in the last analysis rested not on an emotion or even a noble heart but on a feudal concept of service. The Italian poets realized this and turned to metaphysical analysis. Walther von der Vogelweide realized it and removed the essential features of courtliness from his best love poems.

Walther's great service to German love-poetry is his recognition of the futility of *Minnedienst*. To him, true love was mutual and natural. Consequently his lovers meet in a spring landscape which is not the formal description derived from classical rhetoric but a modification of it in which each element is alive. His lady is fresh and young. She is not a lady who must be served but a person who is to be loved naturally and who must return this love. There is no service element in this love, but the existence of the service concept gives many opportunities to contrast natural love with the artificial concepts of *Minnesang*. An excellent example is this passage from the poem "Muget ir schouwen":

> Daz mich, frowe, an fröiden irret,
> daz ist iuwer lîp.
> An iu einer ez mir wirret,
> ungenædic wîp.
> Wâ nemt ir den muot?
> Ir sît doch genâden rîche:
> tuot ir mir ungnædeclîche,
> sô sît ir niht guot.

The strophe is full of references to the clichés of love-service, but they are there only to be mocked. Walther, like his great contemporaries, knew of the existence of a courtly convention but he ceased to believe in it after his apprenticeship, even though in later life he occasionally wrote songs in the mode.

What, then, are we to understand by courtly love in German literature? Firstly, we should think of it in a literal sense, as love-at-court. To this degree German literature, like all literature of the High Middle Ages not written by clerics, is in some sense courtly, because it was written for audiences at courts which thought of themselves as possessing a superior culture. But if we are to think of courtly love as a special kind of love—spiritual, unfulfilled, non-sensual and all the other epithets commonly attributed to it, then in German as in French literature we are faced with very difficult problems. It is clear that German authors regarded the love they found in the works of their French models as characterized by love-service. This is natural enough, since it appears in one form or other in most if not all French romances. That they did not always recognize the irony in Chrétien's treatment is not surprising. A large number of modern critics have failed to recognize it also. This element of service, the most telling evidence of the influence of feudal society on the love concept, was regarded as a thoroughly bad characteristic by the greatest of the German authors. It is in this sense that they recognized "courtly love" and in this sense that they rejected it. There is no German version of Chrétien's *Lancelot*. All the poetry of these authors is a reaction to courtly love, and, in the best authors, it is a rejection. The ideal of love based on service and admiration of specific qualities is to be replaced by mutual attraction. Each in his own way, Wolfram, Gottfried, and Walther told of a love that was shared and in turning his back on the concept of service opened new ways for the consideration of the love phenomenon.

Notes

1. Gustav Ehrismann, "Die Grundlagen des ritterlichen Tugendsystems," *Zeitschrift für Deutsches Altertum und Deutsche Literatur*, LVI (1919), 137–216.

2. Ernst Robert Curtius, "Das ritterliche Tugendsystem," *Deutsche Vierteljahrsschrift für Literaturwissenschaft und Geistesgeschichte*, XXI (1943), 343–68.

3. Eduard Neumann, "Der Streit um das ritterliche Tugendsystem," *Erbe der Vergangenheit*, Festgabe für Karl Helm (Tübingen: Niemeyer, 1951), pp. 137–55.

4. Hartmann von Aue, *Der arme Heinrich*, ed. Fedor Bech (Leipzig: Brockhaus, 1891), lines 47ff.

5. Hans Furstner, *Studien zur Wesensbestimmung der höfischen Minne* (Groningen: Wolters, 1956).

6. *Iwein*, ed. Fedor Bech (Leipzig: Brockhaus, 1873), lines 8121ff.

7. Karl Kurt Klein, "Wolframs Selbstverteidigung," *Zeitschrift für Deutsches Altertum und Deutsche Literatur*, LXXXV (1954–5), 150–62.

8. Gottfried's *Tristan*, trans. A. Hatto (Baltimore: Penguin Books, 1960), p. 145.

9. Herbert Kolb, *Der Begriff der Minne* (Tübingen: Niemeyer, 1958).

10. *PMLA*, LXXVII (1962), 364–72.

11. Hatto, p. 193.

Guenevere, or the Uses of Courtly Love

THEODORE SILVERSTEIN
University of Chicago

The title of my paper is no accident. Its second part arises both from the varieties of modern preoccupation with our theme and, more immediately, from the title of our present conference itself, which, I remind you, is "the *meaning* of courtly love." I am not fully comfortable with the term *meaning*, since it too often means this or that special scheme of interpretation, formalized into a general theory, which a critic erects upon a particular literary work, thinking that schema profound, though it is almost by definition superficial, this is, something superimposed upon the literal *superficies* of a work.

Much of what I have to say on this occasion will turn upon such special concerns and interests, historical, literary, and philosophical, showing in part how they have defined the general field of courtly love and determined some of its various *foci* of interest. Since I have a prejudice in favor of the autonomy and integrity of individual literary objects, as against generalizing and external hypotheses, I hope to suggest how certain theories have affected our reading, sometimes limiting our perception of other aspects of poetry which give immediate form to the subject of love as it occurs in particular poets and poems. And as meaning has come to have a special aura in our time, imparting a peculiar air of mystery or validity to interpretive hypotheses, I prefer the simple operational word *uses*. Those uses are the individual acts of individual critics and also, *haud mire,* of the medieval poets themselves. It is plain, therefore, that my attention will be directed, less to the supposed "truth" about the nature of natures of courtly love or the validity of this or that theory as to its source, than to the ways in which some critics have committed themselves, and to the implications of their commitments for literary interpretation and literary history. So much for my phrase "The Uses of Courtly Love."

The first term in my title, Guenevere, is no simple piece of pretty decoration. She is there because in Arthurian romance she becomes in her person the type of the chivalresque beloved, but a type defined by the particularities of the relationship with her lover Lancelot. Her episode with Modred in Geoffrey of Monmouth and his followers remains in that peculiar descent what it had always been, treachery and sin and Christian penance; it has little moment, except by contrast, for our present discourse. But the events and dilemmas of Chrétien's *Le Chevalier de la Charrette* are quite another matter. They establish in subsequent romance a view of courtly love which for certain modern critics comes close to providing its most distinctive definition. Whatever one may say of love in *Erec and Enid, Cligès, Yvain,* even *Perceval* (and they all differ with respect to love's role and character), or further in the tragedy of Tristan and Isolde, Guenevere and Lancelot sit somewhere near the center. For critics the *De arte honeste amandi* of Andreas Capellanus may seem to be the *Summa theologica* of courtly passion. But if it is that *Summa,* then *Le Chevalier de la Charrette* might pass for love's earliest *Commedia.*

If we were to set in order the concerns of medieval writers with courtly love, whether implicit or explicit in their works, we might express such concerns in the form of three general questions: What is it? How does it proceed? And what are the effects of its practice on the mind and manners of Christian knights and ladies? We too ask those questions in our time, but what was for them a living preoccupation, connected with current problems of morals and of faith and reflected in contemporary poetry and song, is for us an historical pastime. That difference has given several further questions a peculiar importance among modern scholars and critics. Courtly love seems to have flowered most richly in the West and begun its growth in the twelfth, perhaps more precisely in the late eleventh, century, spreading from Provence to the borders of Latin Europe, to Germany, and across the narrow seas to Greater Britain. Why the twelfth century? Why the south of France? And from what source or sources came the seed? These are among the questions that fascinate us now, using up in recent years our searching energies in argument and sometimes in polemics. Quite naturally, the very last of those intriguing questions—from what source or sources?—was not without its medieval interest to authority, which sought to distinguish between the ethos of courtly love and the tenets of the orthodox religion. In similar fashion, the modern critic's interest is not entirely historical, sometimes even not primarily so. Though the phenomena he studies occurred in the distant past, his manipulations may reflect a present vogue, as in the case of those who read the courtly poetry in terms of that current fancy, Myth.

What is courtly love? Its most famous, and for some most provoking, definition in our time is of course C. S. Lewis's, just as Andreas Capellanus provides its most elaborate, explicit medieval definition. Indeed, in Andreas's *De arte honeste amandi* (which I like to render *How to Practice Love and Be a Gentleman*) we get an account of the art from the moment of its rise as a passion in the lover, stimulated by the experience of the eye, to its consummation in virtue and grace; an account which also furnishes, on the way, a psychology, a sociology, a list of rules of conduct, a book of morals and manners with literary models of how to talk of love, an anthology of cases and decisions at law, even an apocalypse in the form of a moral vision of the lovers' other-world. He tells us at what ages love begins and when it ends, differently for men and for women, and who may love and who may not. In this milieu of knights and ladies fencing, the very best of lovers for his distinctive excellence is the cleric, though a nun of course is not to be drawn to the game. Peasants are excluded, since their necessary toil providing our basic nourishment leaves them no leisure for the subtleties of Venus. Hence, should a knight be attracted by a maiden of that class, the usual formal exercises may be suspended in favor of a certain modicum of force in order to overcome the foolish modesty of her kind. This is a book of definitions indeed! Whatever may be Andreas's intention in depicting that theater of special posturing (his Roman model, Ovid, had written his love treatise with irony, and Professor Robertson has described that rhetoric which gives to the *De arte honeste amandi*, as he thinks, its own distinctive *ironia*), whatever, I say, may be the goodly chaplain's intention, the treatise had considerable impact, straight, on subsequent poetry and romance. But seduced by his vision of a world peculiarly available to the social novelist, we, like certain of our medieval ancestors, may find ourselves entangled in its details, its characteristic interests and events, and forget that our problems are also to define, if we can, the basic nature and to find the source or sources of this strange literary current of secular love. Moreover, we are not to fail to remember that we are dealing with a congeries of discrete literary objects, different, it may be, in purpose, in tone, and in organic form.

Entanglement of that sort is, after all, what in fact happens to Chrétien, to Wolfram von Eschenbach, to Geoffrey Chaucer, to the *Gawain* poet, just to name a few—and why not, since they are novelists and poets, not philosophers, apologetes, or critics? In Chrétien the presence of love in a variety of shapes and circumstances provides the range of novelistic problems that his several romances explore: in *Erec* the tension between love and chivalry, but married love and the testing of man and wife together; in *Yvain* a similar tension, but the testing primarily of husband and that in separation from his wife. And in both the question of love is touched by other considerations than passion idealized. In the *Charrette* the lover is pressed to the extreme both by love itself and by the lady, who is his beloved but not his wife; in the *Perceval* the role of mother love becomes an efficient cause in the progress of a knight from secular to spiritual virtue. Throughout all this corpus only the *Charrette* establishes love itself, unchallenged, as the primary force operating on protagonists and events, and that in a form and movement which Marie de Champagne apparently suggested and approved of. To purists like the late Father Denomy only the *Charrette* among the works of Chrétien might be said strictly to deal with courtly love, call the other loves romantic, chivalresque, noble, ideal, or what you will. Such a distinction is substantive for those who have a special theory, historical or philosophic, about the rise to importance of secular love in the West. But Chrétien evidently had no such purist preoccupation. If the *Charrette* delineates an interest of Marie de Champagne, the other romances also deal with love, with secular love, what else? but sensitive and fine in the sensitive and courtly world of chivalry. Are they, or are they not, also aspects of what may be called Courtly Love?

Purist or not, modern critics of *amour courtois* have inevitably involved themselves in the difficult problems of histories and sources. Ovidian poetry and Cluniac devotion, Neo-Platonism and Manichean dualism, Chartrians and Cathari and Arabs: these make up the complex almanac of those who seek to give us love's nativity. That almanac is not merely a conflation of clashing hypotheses about sources; it also records the differences, many of them profound, between their proponents on the very basic nature of courtly love itself. What is primary in it, what are its secondary characteristics? What is its original character, what its later development? What is Christian in it, what un-Christian, what anti-Christian? What is poetic in it, what moralized and—to use the word of Denis de Rougement—degraded? Which of these questions you set out to answer, and the answer that you give, reflect the prejudice with which you treat of courtly love as a phenomenon.

Ovid's place in the game is taken for granted by everyone, for Ovid was the medieval poet of love *par excellence,* but it is a place that has constantly diminished in significance as special theorizing has tended to displace it from the center. However his celebration of the joys of love may have served his medieval disciples as stimulus and model—the concentration on the loved one, the elaborate forms of devotion, the secrecy, the pleasure—, his carnality is said to be radically opposed to the moral and spiritual sublimation of courtly love. How far such opposition does in fact occur is not always clear in the Provençal poets themselves, at least when we look with careful eye at individual cases, unprejudiced by *a priori* theories. If, for example, *fin' amor* is spiritual and fine in the troubadour singer Marcabru, as Dimitri Scheludko has observed, what do you say of his follower and disciple Bernart Marti, whose delight in his beloved is carnal enough—Ovidian in spirit, if you like—and yet, as he tells us, when in the arms of his beloved

Ne de fin' amor aver mais,[1]

he could not get any more from *fin' amor.* Yet the moral of this tale is clear enough: the awareness of a basic opposition, the opposition between carnality and spirit, between passion, if you will, and love, which lies at the foundation of all the distinctive instances of courtly love.

It is that opposition, that tension, if you like, which has beguiled the modern critics and seduced them into tempting explanations. Among those explanations have been the various productions of what are supposed to be the "intellectual background" of courtly love, among which the most constant have been the traditions of neo-Platonism. The value of neo-Platonism as an explanation lies in its dualism of body and soul. The yearning attempt of the soul to escape carnality and rise to a state of rest in its supernatural origin results in an outlook, a process, and a psychology which seem to offer a basis for what, in the view of some critics, lies at the heart of courtly love: that it begins in natural desire, that the beloved is superior to the lover, that it rises beyond carnality to something higher and better, that its desire, constantly self-examining and self-renewed, takes on a characteristic intensity and zeal.

As to how such traditions came to inform and shape the twelfth-century poetry of love, we have almost as many hypotheses as there are critics: Christian neo-Platonism, of course, whose line is St. Augustine and John the Scot, with, for some, Bishop Fulbert and the Chartrians, Heloise and Peter Abaelard in special disseminating roles. To that may be added the moving presence of Bernardine and Cluniac mysticism, whose differentiation between *caritas* and *amor* Scheludko has followed out impressively in the poetry of the troubadours, as analogous to their distinction between *fin' amors* and *amars*, between good love and bad. For others the important special ingredient in the history is the twelfth-century revival of a Manichaean dualism and, related to it, the conspicuous appearance in Provence of Catharist heresy and heretics, by whose asceticism some would like to explain the opposition of courtly love to marriage and its stress on psychological unfulfillment. Finally, for Denomy and those who follow him, there are the poetry and philosophy of the Arabs, whose contacts through the Middle East, Sicily and Spain produced by the beginning of the twelfth century a new and major influence on the minds and hearts of Western Christians.

Of the validity of all or any of these views, how they argue and what they explain, this is not the time to treat in detail. One might be disposed to admit the general relevance of neo-Platonism, though alone it is too general an influence in the West to allow any useful and precise delineation. As to the position of those who have seen in courtly love the qualities of Bernardine *caritas*, Professor Gilson long ago objected that, whatever later relationships might have developed between the two, in origin they must have been quite different in character. The overwhelming sense that that is so lies behind de Rougemont's Catharist hypothesis, and it motivated in part the efforts of Father Denomy to find an Arabic origin for courtly love. But disparity in fundamental character does not necessarily mean difference in literal source. To illustrate with some literary examples of another sort: we may recognize that those two outrageous specimens of satire, the Gospel of Marks of Silver and the Testament of the Nuns of Rémiremont, are basically divergent from the Christian works they parody, without pursuing recondite philosophies to explain the point of their literary joking!

Of Denomy's efforts I have little further to say at the moment. I aired my views of them some years ago and would only add now that, despite my earlier objections on both theoretical and historical grounds, they seem to me at present to have a more permanent value, not so much for the special intellectual setting they propose, but for calling our attention to some of those collections of subject-matter, attitudes, language and devices relevant to love which the two bodies of poetry possess in common. That in the end may be the most important value of many other such studies, their observation and accumulation of shared conventions, rather than their special theories of significance or their particular accounts of genesis, accounts that signal too often a circumscribed and myopic enterprise. Such is the suggestion of the recent study by Mr. Peter Dronke, *Medieval Latin and the Rise of European Love-Lyric*, which finds a greater unity in medieval poetry of love than the purist views of courtly love permit us to observe, and then goes on to bring together a body of that poetry's conventions, not merely from France and Germany, from the Arabs and from Christian Spain, but from ancient Egypt, Byzantium, Persia, Georgia, Iceland, and Greek Italy. This is a widening out indeed

83

in time and space! It calls to our attention, importantly for the present occasion, the fact that whatever role *amour courtois* might have played in the West, it did not develop in isolation from a broader tradition of secular love poetry which flourished quite healthily beside it, and it was not uniquely or even primarily the cause or form of that poetry's rise and spread in the eleventh and twelfth centuries and afterwards.

Of all the modern accounts of love which make peculiar use of *amour courtois*, the one by Denis de Rougemont is perhaps the most provocative, and that for a number of reasons. On the one hand, he belongs with all those who have pursued along strange paths the "source" of courtly love, but his speciality, Catharist heresy, also mirrors a bewitchment, already well begun in the nineteenth century, with the supposed operation in history of odd suppressed sects and secret heresies. On the other hand, he also falls among those critics for whom the significance, indeed the magic, of poetry resides in a primordial myth. In different ways Jessie Weston and Robert Graves are in that company, as are also such other interpreters of courtly romances as Charles Bertram Lewis, Ananda K. Coomaraswamy and Antoinette Fierz-Monnier. Jesse Weston follows the Frazerian myth of the king-priest who dies and lives, Bertram Lewis the Greek myths of Theseus and the Springs of Dodona; for Graves the myth is the myth of the be-witching White Goddess—and that myth is for him a definition of poetry. Ananda Coomaraswamy goes back to the Indra myth, which, founded in the themes of unity and diversity, reflects that *philosophia perennis* which gives their real meaning to subsequent literatures, as far as their specimens can be made to recall it; and Mme. Fierz-Monnier gets tangled up in psychological myths and Jung.

De Rougemont's basic myth is Tristan and Isolde, from which he draws his argument on love. That myth, in terms of its literal events, is the story of the two unfortunate lovers, and is Celtic in its genetic connections; in terms of its psychological origin it deals with the mystery of the supreme power of passion, a passion which overrides marriage and all normal reality, even the love of lovers for each other, a passion which becomes the love of love itself and whose necessary outcome is death. In terms of the way story-tellers and poets naturalized this theme in its narrative, magic and the code of chivalry become the symbolic means. Such a myth is essentially a poetic conception, touched by primordial emotions, and like other myths it is a construct of the critic's. For myths, by definition, are not the literary objects which contain them, but must be extracted by some process of analysis from literature. The process frequently plays hob with the form and order, the internal economy, if you like, of individual literary pieces and often overlooks the facts of chronology. When de Rougemont talks of the myth of Tristan and Isolde, we are never sure when he is using Thomas, when Béroul, or even when Richard Wagner. Yet if a piece at some point runs counter to his views, he can speak of its author thus, as he does of Thomas:

Thomas . . . is driven to making passion less inhuman and hence more tolerable to a moralist. Inferior in this respect to Béroul, he is the first writer to *degrade* the myth.[2]

This observation of de Rougemont's reminds us of one very common consequence of criticism of this sort: the critics tend to be a sort of literary *peelers;* that is, they proceed by stripping down a poem of all its individual traits until they have exposed, as they think, its essential core or kernel. When they are sensitive to the poetic craft, as is Robert Graves, they value the skill of the poet and the special conventions within which that poet works. When the critics are less responsive to artistry, then they may assert, as do Bertram Lewis and Coomaraswamy, that poetry obscures what is really significant and poets may even be the enemies of truth; or, as does Mme. Fierz-Monnier, that individual artistry is insignificant. Let the writer, any writer, by some accident fall upon and use the symbols of the myths of the collective imagination and he produces a masterpiece *willy-nilly*.

De Rougemont does not fall into any such traps, but his double preoccupation, the myth of primordial love and the Catharist transformation, produces its inevitable effects; a judgment of art if not of artistry. Not only in his alleged degradation of the myth is Thomas inferior to Béroul, but Chrétien in the *Charrette* was writing at Marie de Champagne's behest on something he did not really understand; whereas Gottfried von Strassburg, who knew whereof he wrote (*i.e.,* the Catharist mysteries), was able to produce a more significant piece.

What saves de Rougemont in the end (let us close our eyes for the moment to the Cathari), what saves him from such simplistic and infatuated views as those of Fierz-Monnier and Coomaraswamy, is exactly a sense for the serious claims of poetry. In the case of a more recent lover of love, Mr. John Broadbent, the tension between passion and love is virtually all his argument, producing that dialectic of opposites which, when properly resolved, makes what for him is valid in love poetry. Let the resolution be wrong and it degrades the poetry into moralizing and even allegory, and that, according to Broadbent, is the sorry fate of medieval courtly writing, whether Chrétien's, the *Roman de la rose*, or some other misdirected effort than these.

For certain critics, not bound to origins or special cases, the history of courtly love in the writings which contain them is not one of decay but development and sometimes simply one of difference. What was true for Provence was not always true for Germany, what held in the twelfth century was not the case in the fourteenth or the fifteenth. Courtly love was not everywhere opposed to marriage. Its literary ideals became more formalized, in step, as it were, with the literary formalization of the "code" of chivalry, as that code drew, not simply on local rules and regulations, but also on the Aristotelian ethics, transformed by Cicero and Seneca, and expressed in such works as the *Moralium dogma philosophorum*, and sometimes, it is true, reduced to metaphoric formula in the moral ballades of Eustache Deschamps, the poetry of tournaments, and heraldry. It also on its way produced some critical Christian confrontations, whose masterpieces include, not only the Vulgate Cycle of Arthurian romance, but so moving and magical a piece as the prose *High History of the Holy Grail*. To be committed to a theory of degradation and decay may put too high a value on a view of passionate love, too little on the profound power of great poetry.

By now I hope it is clear why I have employed the term the *uses* of courtly love. The uses of the term have been so manifold and its histories so many, that patently you can get almost anything you want out of the subject. What you get depends very largely on what has come to be known as your approach. One response to the frustrating variety of views which that condition has produced is a growing persuasion in the world *post* C. S.

Lewis that courtly love, as a viable entity, never existed except in the minds of modern critics, that the "code" is a piece of Victorian sentimentalism, and that the term itself, in a sense the reinvention of Gaston Paris, has by now come to do more harm than good.

Perhaps our critical task is, not to ask which hypothesis is "true," which approach is an impediment to another approach, nor to face each other in polemical opposition, each defending his system or his "school" from every other; nor simply to abandon term and concept together in a grand and purifying holocaust. Perhaps we need, for courtly love as for other themes and questions, a systematic critique of the natures of positions, estimating what the consequences are of each, but more important still, what are its powers and its limits. Since four-fold schemes seem to have a peculiar witchery in our time, let me suggest a four-fold schema of my own for classifying the intellectual orientation and methodological procedures of the critics of courtly love. No critic necessarily employs any one of the four exclusively, though each may be placed essentially in one of its categories.

The first we may call Grammatical, also Descriptive or even Conventional. Essentially it collects and describes the characteristic conventions of the courtly love poetry. It has always been an ingredient in the critical history of the subject, but especially in the earlier and less contentious stages. Peter Dronke is perhaps its most successful current practitioner.

The second we may denominate Dialectical. It stresses the themes of opposition, tension, and resolution. Many histories proceed in this fashion; it is the method, for example, of de Bruyne in his history of medieval esthetics. For the poetry of love de Rougement and, especially, Broadbent provide instances.

The third kind may be called Rhetorical, or Moral or Ideational. Here we may place all those accounts which stress the themes of intellectual or psychological truth, moral idealization, and allegorical significance. The critical range runs all the way from Coomaraswamy to the methods and aims of certain of my colleagues at the present conference.

The fourth kind of criticism we may call Poetic, or Esthetic. This should deal with how courtly love functions as an organic constituent of an artistic object or whole, as an essential element in the internal economy of a piece, affecting and affected by its other parts. Though many critics have, in effect, practised this kind sporadically, few have been formally aware of its fuller and significant possibilities. Even history, as some critics will wish to use it to prove or disprove the "real" existence of courtly love, is not simply literal social history, but itself varies in kind, hence in results.

Let me add that there are many other ways of cutting the cake, but the essential point is that we should find some device, instead of that of mutual self-defence, for seeing our own approach, as well as that of others, with the kind of intellectual detachment which may lead to critical rather than merely polemical confrontation and resolution.

I now come quickly to my conclusion. Some eighteen years ago I wrote a piece on courtly love, the occasion for which was the appearance of Father Denomy's fresh and stimulating studies, and it dealt especially with what he suggested were its Arabic parallels and sources.[3] In the course of that piece I found myself surveying other views as well, and it was largely as a summary of such views that some readers found my essay valuable. But it was not a summary, though there was summary in it; nor was it merely a criticism of Denomy, though it criticized his position; nor did it propose a serious Christian alternative to Denomy's Arabs or to any other account of the sources, though it did pretend to offer a current Christian counterpart to some of the principles in Avicenna's Arabic treatise, the *Risalah fil Ishk*, which Denomy had advanced in evidence for his case. What my essay presented, in the end, was an argument, an argument on the narrowing effect of all such concentration on intellectual backgrounds and sources, together with a call for other sorts of studies, literary and critical, turned to individual works, in which courtly love might be an element, but disciplined and made immediately relevant to the particular intrinsic issues of each piece. And this is still, I submit, what we can do.

The particular Christian neo-Platonic source that I proposed, to balance against the *Risalah fil Ishk* was a construct of my own, based on actual materials from history, but with certain liberties which I allowed myself to take. In the context of my argument it was a piece of irony, intended to criticize those other sources that successive scholars brought forward to "explain" courtly love, and in the process each would find in what is, after all, a very complex phenomenon, those details most significant which his sources seemed to single out. That construct, as I said quite plainly in my essay, was never intended to be taken as a source, though in fact it has been read as if that were my intention. More recently in a piece on *Gawain and the Green Knight* I argued that too much effort has been spent by scholarship tracking down supposed material sources of the poem and too little on other kinds of problems. Even should we find, I there contended, an earlier poem on Gawain and the Green Knight (*De Galvaneo et milite viride*, let us suppose), it would not necessarily make a serious difference in the artistic accomplishment of the English *Gawain* poet. There, too, I lightly proposed what such an earlier poem might have been like and invented some of its lines and even the name of its poet, Petrus Argenteus—all in a statement that I thought said exactly what I was doing.[4] That piece of irony, read straight by an unobservant reader, now appears as a serious hypothesis in an account of my essay in a current Arthurian journal. Petrus Argenteus, I'm afraid, simply means me.

Well, I am warned by now, and so I now warn you, as I come to a close with the little literary flourish that the occasion may permit.

The uses of courtly love have been legion among scholars and critics alike in the last half century and more. In recent years the tournament frenzy has somewhat abated but not ceased, and the present conference is testimony that the game is bound to go on at a reasonably lively pace, though the rules of the game and even the game itself may change. We can imagine some curious visitor in the spectators' pavilion asking, "How long, O lord? with what new turns? and why?" He might ask all this in the words of *Tristan and Isolde:*

> Amors par force vos demeine.
> Conbien durra vostre folie?
> Trop avez mene ceste vie.

Which, being paraphrased, means:

The force of love is strong.
Your fit will last how long?
Too far you've wandered wrong.

And my favorite fictitious medieval poet can be imagined as having said it equally well in his particular pig Latin:

Domina vi dominavit.
Diu stultum perduravit.
Stultus errat qui amavit.

To which from knight and scholar alike will come the answer of
the ages:

Si longuement l'avon menee
Itel fu nostre destinee.

Or as the *Gawain* poet says in such English as he can:

Of destines derf & dere
What may mon do bot fonde?

But even earlier than this, and once again with feeling:

De sortibus obscuris
Quid fortibus ni duris
Se mittant adventuris?

SIC DIXIT PETRUS ARGENTEUS.

Notes

1. *Les poésies de Bernart Marti*, ed. Ernest Hoepffner, Classiques français du moyen âge, 61 (Paris, 1929), p. 31.

2 *Love in the Western World* (New York: Harcourt, Brace, 1956), p. 38, note.

3. "Andreas, Plato, and the Arabs: Remarks on Some Recent Accounts of Courtly Love," *Modern Philology*, XLVII (1949–50), 117–26.

4. Theodore Silverstein, "*Sir Gawain*, Dear Brutus, and Britain's Fortunate Founding: A Study in Comedy and Convention," *Modern Philology*, LXII (1964–65), 189–206.

Discussion

The Conference concluded with a round-table discussion among the participants. It was chaired by Professor Bernard F. Huppé, of the State University of New York at Binghamton. A somewhat condensed transcription of the discussion follows.

MR. HUPPÉ:

Let me start the discussion with a question for Professor Robertson. You talked about *The Book of the Duchess* and indicated what an obstruction any concept of courtly love was in dealing with that poem. But I'm wondering about the passage in which the Black Knight talks about Blanche as not being the kind of woman who sends men to the far reaches of the earth,

> into Walakye,
> To Pruyse, and into Tartarye,
> To Alysaundre, ne into Turkye,
> And byd hym faste anoon that he
> Goo hoodles to the Drye Se
> And come hom by the Carrenar,
> And seye, 'Sir, be now ryght war
> That I may be of yow here seyn
> Worshyp, or that ye come ageyn!'
> She ne used no such knakkes smale.

It seems to me that unless you have a tradition of courtly love, a literary convention such as Professor Jackson talks about, those lines are almost meaningless.

Mr. ROBERTSON:

Well, I think that what Chaucer is saying—or, rather, what the Black Knight is saying—about Blanche is that she is a reasonable and sensible lady who does not impose outrageous tasks on people who come to her as suitors. Now it is further said about this lady that her eyes seem to say "Mercy," and some fools think that is what they are saying, the fools being those who think they are going to get some sort of physical mercy from the lady. I don't doubt that women in the Middle Ages sometimes did as much as they could to get some sort of service from men. Women are still doing the same thing, can still be as demanding of service, but we don't call such behavior "courtly love."

Mr. SILVERSTEIN:

It's true that women require service of men to this day, but the kinds of service are quite different from those required in the Middle Ages. Certainly I would like to define courtly love as involving a range of things, including even the formalized characteristics of feudal service. Now Mr. Robertson feels that he has to destroy the very notion of courtly love in order to establish a probability that certain kinds of arguments are what we need to re-interpret *The Book of the Duchess* and *Troilus and Criseyde*. It may very well be that these poems should be re-interpreted—I think he has presented a very good preliminary case—but I don't think that this entails denying the presence of literary conventions that, in one sense or another, we call "courtly love." Chaucer did not need to disbelieve in all the conventions of courtly love in order to give an ironic, or moralistic, account of the behavior of the Black Knight.

Mr. HUPPÉ:

Professor Jackson, would you like to comment?

Mr. JACKSON:

Thank you. Let me make clear that I am as much against the use of "courtly love" as a blanket term as anyone else. I have spent a lot of my life—as we all have—giving my low opinion of Lewis's *Allegory of Love*. It's a charmingly seductive book that has led many a fair young man astray. "Courtly love" is an absolutely useless phrase, if by it we suggest that every romance and lyric from William IX to Chaucer displays one or another variant of courtly love. But, on the other hand, I refuse to believe that so many people could have tried, in lyric and romance, to arrive at some definition of a very particular kind of love unless they felt that this love was different from mere attraction between the sexes. Why all the questions about what *fin' amors* was? Why should so many German lyric poets have begun their poems with the words, "Saget mir ieman, waz ist minne?" What *is* it? If it was mere attraction between the sexes why bother to go into it? And furthermore, I also want to know why love is so often regarded as an intellectual exercise, an exercise in definition and substantiation which ultimately becomes metaphysical in nature. All of this seems to me to show that there was a feeling among literary men, and also among the members of the small audience which listened to them and could understand them, that there was a kind of love which was special. This love required understanding and even definition. But I don't think it was the same in Chrétien as in Bernart de Ventadorn, nor even the same in Heinrich von Morungen as in his contemporary Walther von der Vogelweide. One more point, on the question of literary convention. I would emphasize that the very word *knight* had a different meaning in literature from that which it had in practice. Why otherwise would we have the celebrated Provençal *tenso* between a knight and a king in which it is firmly established that the knight is the better man? It is up to the king to overcome the problem of being a king and to show that he can be as good as a knight. Knighthood does not simply make a man an armed retainer, not even a member of a particular social class; it endows him with particular virtues. Now by the 14th century, the time of Chaucer, such views were things of the past, historical and archaic. They were being re-evaluated as a historical phenomenon, not as something which had just evolved and was still eminently discussable as a living thing.

MR. BENTON:

It seems to me that the human activities we have been discussing—insofar as we have been discussing real human actions—are describable in *medieval* terminology. For example, yesterday Professor Jackson spoke to us about a German reaction. It was a reaction against something, and I think that something is set forth with perfect clarity in the *Lai dou lecheor*, when the ladies discuss why men fight in tournaments and do brave deeds. It is to be expected that a moral person would "react" against the kind of love the ladies discuss. I don't think we need any other term for it than Aquinas's—the love of concupiscence. Of course people pursued concupiscent love, and they also had a literature and literary conventions about such love. This should not be a problem for us.

MR. SINGLETON:

I think I'm going to agree with the assertion of Professor Robertson that the notion of courtly love is an impediment to the understanding of medieval texts. But I want to go further and say that history misused is a very great impediment to the understanding of *any* literary text. It matters everything where you set yourself up. I got a great deal from Mr. Benton's paper but I want to argue a point or two with him. I already knew, perhaps we all did, that seducers were flogged through the streets of medieval cities. The fact gets into a note in my commentary on Canto XVII of *Inferno*, in which Jason, among other seducers, is flogged around a circle in Hell. Let this be an instance of how a historian can deliver up to someone who is reading a text a very significant detail. But it is one thing to be concerned with reading a poem and taking from history whatever help history can give, and quite another thing to set yourself up with "courtly love"—or whatever you are going to name it—as a preconception and then proceed to test it on the text. You set yourself up inside or outside of the poem and that original position, or posture, seems to me to make all the difference in the world. The verification of hypotheses in history is not the reading of poetry, which is what I happen to be interested in. I remember the first graduate course I ever took was on Boccaccio's *Decameron* and we literally did not read or discuss a single story of the *Decameron*. We spent half of the time talking about the sources of the *Decameron* and the rest of the time talking about its influence. Now the battle against this sort of thing was won long ago and I am aware that younger minds are dissatisfied with the style of the victors. They are not satisfied with "the poem in itself," but are determined to bring poems into a social context. They are insisting on the *engagement* of the poem, the involvement of the literary work in history. They are less like the old literary historians than like contemporary sociologists, and often they seem to be fixing the poem in a frame that amounts—for me—to an impediment to reading.

MR. SILVERSTEIN:

You raise some basic critical problems. On the whole, I think that the contrast of positions that you describe is a false dichotomy. I am reminded of that other controversy, when we went around the MLA convention asking our friends whether they were scholars or critics. But let me leave that and return to something you said in your paper. You suggested that, to the orthodox, the elevation of Beatrice was "scandalous," and then you went on to defend her rôle by using the notion of play. I think that that is a very good way to talk about fictions, but I want to add that there are two different ways of forming fictions, two different games to play. Dante's is a philosophical poem, but he gives us Beatrice, not Noys. His fiction is philosophical, but it's unlike that of Bernardus Silvestris or Alanus de Insulis. Alanus, for instance, never puts in the poem anything that looks like an ordinary human being. His fiction is pure *psychomachia* (I use the term only as a shorthand). For the state of mind attuned to that kind of philosophical poetry Beatrice may indeed have been scandalous, but so is every other Florentine, every other historical figure, in the *Comedy*. Dante gives us not *psychomachia* allegory, but exemplary fiction in which the didactic intent is fixed within a fiction that seems like history.

MR. ROBERTSON:

I must say that I am not quite so impressed with the "scandal" of Beatrice as I might be. Increased exemplification is a characteristic of late medieval style; we have instances of actual persons used in an exemplary way even in the *Roman de la rose*. And the Italians might be expected to be a little keener at this sort of thing than anyone else. From a stylistic point of view their art was quite advanced. They had a sharper awareness of the literal surfaces of things. They were more interested than others in surface appearance. I don't mean by this that they were not interested in significance, but that they favored—stylistically—a very high degree of exemplification. But to return to the wider question: I don't think it is really possible to understand a work of literature outside of its cultural setting. I doubt, for example, that it is possible to understand a surrealist poem unless you know something about the atmosphere of Europe between the two wars. I doubt that Chaucer, had he been able to read one, would have understood a surrealist poem at all, however great it might be as a poem. I have a suspicion that in the Middle Ages poems *per se* did not really exist, and I therefore dislike trying to talk about "the poem as poem." It is much more fruitful to study poetry in its historical context, as I tried to yesterday in discussing the *Troilus*. I think that we should as best we can seek to recover—though it's an impossible task to perform perfectly—the attitudes, the intellectual environment or cultural context that produced the work of art in the first place. The trouble with the notion of courtly love—to return to our starting point—is not that it involves history, but that so much of the "history" connected with it is fictitious.

Mr. Jackson:

Let me add one remark on an aspect of the social context of medieval love poetry that we haven't touched on, and that is the rather crude question of flattery. I happen to hold the view that much Provençal poetry, however refined it may have later become, started off as good straight-forward flattery written by professionals who knew which side their bread was buttered on. But in quite a short time what was bread and butter poetry in, we'll say, 1130 had become metaphysical by 1230 in certain circles. I exaggerate here, but I want to make the point that a set of consciously held values, or established mores, at one point in time can lead directly to rather different, even opposed, values. The terminology can remain the same, but the meanings differ.

Following this colloquy the panelists responded to a number of questions from the audience, after which Mr. Huppé called upon Mr. Jackson to read a "recently discovered fragment" of verse that deserves publication alongside the works of Petrus Argenteus, and will also serve as the epigraph of the conference:

> Amor curialis est infernus non coelestis
> Qui affliget homines semper tam quam pestis.

A Selected Bibliography
of the Theory of Courtly Love

This list is by no means exhaustive. It is limited to secondary sources and emphasizes work done in the last twenty years; older material is included only if particularly noteworthy for one reason or another. Books and articles dealing with individual authors, and only incidentally with Courtly Love, have not been listed. It was compiled by the editor and Prof. Robin Oggins of the State University of New York at Binghamton.

ANDREAS CAPELLANUS. *The Art of Courtly Love*, trans. John Jay Parry. New York: Columbia University Press, 1941.

ASKEW, MELVIN W. "Courtly Love: Neurosis as Institution," *Psychoanalytic Review*, LII (1965), 19–29.

AXHAUSEN, KÄTE. *Die Theorien über den Ursprung der provenzalischen Lyrik*. Marburg: G. H. Nolte, 1937.

BAGLEY, C. P. "Courtly Love-Songs in Galicia and Provence," *Forum for Modern Language Studies*, II (1966), 74–88.

BELPERRON, PIERRE. *La "joie d'amour;" Contribution à l'étude des troubadours et de l'amour courtois*. Paris: Plon, 1948.

BENTON, JOHN F. "The Court of Champagne as a Literary Center," *Speculum*, XXXVI (1961), 551–91.

———. "The Evidence for Andreas Capellanus Re-Examined Again," *Studies in Philology*, LIX (1962), 471–78.

BETZ, WERNER. "Andreas Capellanus und der Minnesang," *Unterscheidung und Bewahrung: Festschrift . . . Kunisch*, eds. Klaus Lazarowicz and Wolfgang Kron. Berlin: Walther de Gruyter, 1961, pp. 16–19.

BEZZOLA, RETO R. *Les origines et la formation de la littérature courtoise en Occident (500–1200)*. 3 vols. in 5. Paris: E. Champion, 1944–63.

BIZET, J.-A. *Suso et le minnesang; ou, la morale de l'amour courtois*. Paris: Aubier, 1948.

Bowra, C. M. *Mediaeval Love-Song*. London: Athlone, 1961.

Briffault, Robert S. *The Troubadours*, ed. Lawrence F. Koons. Bloomington: Indiana University Press, 1965.

Broadbent, J. B. *Poetic Love*. London: Chatto and Windus, 1964.

Camproux, Charles. *Joy d'amor (Jeu et joie d'amour)*. Montpellier: Causse et Castelnau, 1965.

Closs, August. "Minnesang and its Spiritual Background," *Medusa's Mirror: Studies in German Literature*, pp. 43–56. London: Cresset, 1957.

Cluzel, Irénée-Marcel. "Les jarÿas et l'amour courtois," *Cultura neolatina*, XX (1960), 233–50.

Coppin, Joseph. *Amour et mariage dans la littérature française du Nord au moyen-âge*. Paris: Librairie d'Argences, 1961.

Crosland, Jessie. "Ovid's Contribution to the Conception of Love known as 'L'Amour courtois,'" *Modern Language Review*, XLII (1947), 199–206.

Davenson, Henri [H.-I. Marrou]. *Les troubadours*. Paris: Éditions du Seuil, 1961.

Denomy, A. J. "Concerning the Accessibility of Arabic Influences to the Earliest Provençal Troubadours," *Mediaeval Studies*, XV (1953), 147–58.

———. "Courtly Love and Courtliness," *Speculum*, XXVIII (1953), 44–63.

———. "The *De Amore* of Andreas Capellanus and the Condemnation of 1277," *Mediaeval Studies*, VIII (1946), 107–49.

———. "*Fin' Amors*: the Pure Love of the Troubadours, Its Amorality, and Possible Source," *Mediaeval Studies*, VII (1945), 139–207.

———. *The Heresy of Courtly Love*. New York: D. X. McMullen, 1947.

———. "An Inquiry into the Origins of Courtly Love," *Mediaeval Studies*, VI (1944), 175–260.

———. "*Jois* Among the Early Troubadours: Its Meaning and Possible Source," *Mediaeval Studies*, XIII (1951), 177–217.

———. "*Jovens*: the Notion of Youth among the Troubadours, its Meaning and Source," *Mediaeval Studies*, XI (1949), 1–22.

Donaldson, E. Talbot. "The Myth of Courtly Love," *Ventures*, V, 2 (1965), 16–23.

Dragonetti, R. "Trois motifs de la lyrique courtoise confrontés avec les *Arts d'aimer*," *Romanica Gandensia*, VII (1959), 5–48.

Dronke, Peter. "Guillaume IX and Courtoisie," *Romanische Forschungen*, LXXIII (1961), 327–38.

———. *Medieval Latin and the Rise of European Love-Lyric*. 2 vols. Oxford: Clarendon, 1965–66.

Errante, Guido. *Marcabru e le fonti sacre dell'antica lirica romanza*. Firenze: G. C. Sansoni, 1948.

———. "Old Provençal Poetry, Latin and Arabic Influences," *Thought*, XX (1945), 305–30.

Fisher, J. H. "Tristan and Courtly Adultery," *Comparative Literature*, IX (1957), 150–64.

Fleming, John V. "The Moral Reputation of the *Roman de la Rose* Before 1400," *Romance Philology*, XVIII (1964–65), 430–35.

FOSTER, KENELM. *Courtly Love and Christianity.* Aquinas Paper, 39. London: Aquin, 1963.

FRANK, DON K. "The Corporeal, the Derogatory, and the Stress on Equality in Andreas' *De Amore*," *Medievalia et Humanistica,* XVI (1964), 30–38.

———. "On the Troubadour *Fin' Amors*," *Romance Notes,* VII (1965–66), 209–17.

FRAPPIER, JEAN. "Vues sur les conceptions courtoises dans les littératures d'oc et d'oïl au XIIᵉ siècle," *Cahiers de civilisation médiévale,* II (1959), 135–56.

FRINGS, THEODOR. *Die Anfänge der europäischen Liebes-Dichtung im 11. und 12. Jahrhundert.* München: Bayerischen Akademie der Wissenschaften, 1960.

FURSTNER, HANS. *Studien zur Wesensbestimmung der höfischen Minne.* Groningen: J. B. Wolters, 1956.

GIBSON, M. CARL. "Background to the Theory of Arabic Origins," *Brigham Young University Studies,* IV (1962), 219–34.

GILLESPIE, GERALD. "Origins of Romance Lyrics: A Review of Research," *Yearbook of Comparative and General Literature,* XVI (1967), 16–32.

GILSON, ETIENNE. *La théologie mystique de saint Bernard.* Études de philosophie médiévale, 20. Paris: J. Vrin, 1934.

GOLDIN, FREDERICK. *The Mirror of Narcissus in the Courtly Love Lyric.* Ithaca: Cornell University Press, 1967.

GORCY, G. " 'Courtois' et 'courtoisie' d'après quelques textes du Moyen Français," *Bulletin des jeunes romanistes,* IV (1961), 15–25.

GREEN, R. H. "Courtly Love," *New Catholic Encyclopedia,* IV, 393–99. New York: McGraw-Hill, 1967.

GRUNEBAUM, GUSTAVE E. VON. "Avicenna's *Risâla fī ᵓl-ᶜišq* and Courtly Love," *Journal of Near Eastern Studies,* XI (1952), 233–38.

HEGER, KLAUS. *Die bisher veröffentlichten Harǧas und ihre Deutungen.* Beihefte zur Zeitschrift für romanische Philologie, 101. Tübingen: Niemeyer, 1960.

ISBĂŞESCU, MIHAIL. *Minne und Liebe: Ein Beitrag zur Begriffsdeutung und Terminologie des Minnesangs.* Tübinger germanistische Arbeiten, 27. Stuttgart: Kohlhammer, 1940.

JACKSON, W. T. H. "The *De amore* of Andreas Capellanus and the Practice of Love at Court," *Romanic Review,* XLIX (1958), 243–51.

KELLY, AMY. *Eleanor of Aquitaine and the Four Kings.* Cambridge, Massachusetts: Harvard University Press, 1950.

KESTING, PETER. *Maria-Frouwe: Über den Einfluss der Marienverehrung auf den Minnesang bis Walther von der Vogelweide.* Medium Aevum: Philologische Studien, 5. München: W. Fink, 1965.

KIRBY, THOMAS A. *Chaucer's Troilus: A Study in Courtly Love.* University, Louisiana: Louisiana State University Press, 1940.

KNUDSON, CHARLES AND JEAN MISRAHI, "Courtly Love" in *The Medieval Literature of Western Europe,* ed. J. H. Fisher, pp. 150–52. New York: New York University Press, 1966.

KOENIGSBERG, RICHARD A. "Culture and the Unconscious Fantasy: Observations on Courtly Love," *Psychoanalytical Review*, LIV (1967), 36–50.

KÖHLER, ERICH. "Observations historiques et sociologiques sur la poésie des troubadours," *Cahiers de civilisation médiévale*, VII (1964), 27–51.

———. *Trobadorlyrik und höfischer Roman*. Neue Beiträge zur Literaturwissenschaft, 15. Berlin: Rütten and Loening, 1962.

KOLB, HERBERT. *Der Begriff der Minne und das Entstehen der höfischen Lyrik*. Hermaea: Germanistische Forschungen, 4. Tübingen: Niemeyer, 1958.

LAFITTE-HOUSSAT, JACQUES. *Troubadours et cours d'amour*. 3rd ed. Paris: Presses universitaires de France, 1966.

LAWLOR, JOHN, ed. *Patterns of Love and Courtesy; Essays in Memory of C. S. Lewis*. Evanston: Northwestern University Press, 1966.

LAZAR, MOSHÉ. *Amour courtois et "fin'amors" dans la littérature du XIIe siècle*. Paris: C. Klincksieck, 1964.

———. "Classification des thèmes amoureux et des images poétiques dans l'oeuvre de Bernard de Ventadour," *Filologia romanza*, VI (1959), 371–400.

———. "Les éléments constitutifs de la 'cortezia' dans la lyrique des troubadours," *Studi mediolatini e volgari*, VI-VII (1958–59), 67–96.

———. "L'idéologie et la casuistique de la *fin'amors*," *Filologia e letteratura*, VIII (1962), 253–73, 380–407.

LEHMANN, ANDRÉE. *Le Rôle de la femme dans l'histoire de France au Moyen-âge*. Paris: Berger-Levrault, 1952.

Lejeune, Rita. "Formules féodales et style amoureux chez Guillaume IX d'Aquitaine," *Atti del VIIIo congresso internazionale di studi romanzi*, II, 227–48. Firenze: Sansoni, 1959.

———. "Rôle littéraire de la famille d'Aliénor d'Aquitaine," *Cahiers de civilisation médiévale*, I (1958), 319–37.

———. "Rôle littéraire d'Aliénor d'Aquitaine et de sa famille," *Cultura neolatina*, XIV (1954), 5–57.

LEWIS, C. S. *The Allegory of Love*. Oxford: Clarendon, 1936.

LOT-BORODINE, MYRRHA. *De l'amour profane à l'amour sacré*. Paris: Nizet, 1961.

MAHONEY, JOHN F. "The Evidence for Andreas Capellanus in Re-Examination," *Studies in Philology*, LV (1958), 1–6.

MARROU, H.-I. "Au dossier de l'amour courtois," *Revue du moyen âge latin*, III (1947), 81–89.

MATHEW, GERVASE. "Marriage and *Amour Courtois* in Late Fourteenth-Century England," *Essays Presented to Charles Williams*. Oxford: Oxford University Press, 1947.

MENÉNDEZ PIDAL RAMÓN. "La primitiva lírica europea: estado actual del problema," *Revista de filología española*, XLIII (1960), 279–354.

MOLLER, HERBERT. "The Meaning of Courtly Love," *Journal of American Folklore*, LXXIII (1960), 39–52.

———. "The Social Causation of the Courtly Love Complex," *Comparative Studies in Society and History*, I (1958–59), 137–63.

MORET, ANDRÉ. "Qu'est-ce que la Minne? Contribution à l'étude de la terminologie et de la mentalité courtoises," *Études Germaniques*, IV (1949), 1–12.

NARDI, BRUNO. "Filosofia dell'amore nei rimatori italiani del Duecento e in Dante," *Dante e la cultura medievale*, Biblioteca di cultura moderna, no. 368. 2nd ed., pp. 1–92. Bari: Laterza, 1949.

NELLI, RENÉ. *L'érotique des troubadours*. Bibliothèque méridionale, 2ᵉ sér., t.38. Toulouse: É. Privat, 1963.

NOLTING-HAUFF, ILSE. *Die Stellung der Liebeskasuistik im höfschen Roman*. Heidelberger Forschungen, 6. Heidelberg: C. Winter, 1959.

NYKL, A. R. *Hispano-Arabic Poetry and its Relations with the Old Provençal Troubadours*. Baltimore: J. H. Furst, 1946.

PALUMBO, PIETRO. "La questione della *Reprobatio amoris* nel trattato di Andrea Cappellano," *Saggi e ricerche in memoria di Ettore Li Gotti*. Centro di studi filogogici e linguistici siciliani, Bollettino, 7. Palermo, 1962, II, 429–46.

PARIS, GASTON. Études sur les romans de la Table Ronde. Lancelot du Lac. II. Le *Conte de la Charrette*," *Romania*, XII (1883), 459–534.

PELLEGRINI, SILVIO. "Intorno al vassallaggio d'amore nei primi trovatori," *Cultura neolatina*, IV-V (1944–45), 21–36.

POLLMANN, LEO. "Dichtung und Liebe bei William von Aquitanien," *Zeitschrift für romanische Philologie*, LXXVIII (1962), 326–57.

———. *Die Liebe in der hochmittelalterlichen Literatur Frankreichs*. Frankfurt a.M.: Klostermann, 1966.

REMY, PAUL. "Les 'cours d'amour': légende et réalité," *Revue de l'Université de Bruxelles*, VII (1954–55), 179–97.

ROBERTSON, D. W., JR. "Chrétien's *Cligés* and the Ovidian Spirit," *Comparative Literature*, VII (1955), 32–42.

———. "The Doctrine of Charity in Medieval Literary Gardens: A Topical Approach through Symbolism and Allegory," *Speculum*, XXVI (1951), 24–49.

———. *A Preface to Chaucer*. Princeton: Princeton University Press, 1962.

———. "The Subject of the *De Amore* of Andreas Capellanus." *Modern Philology*, L (1952–53), 145–61.

ROUGEMONT, DENIS DE. *L'amour et l'Occident*. Paris: Plon, 1939. Translated by Montgomery Belgion as *Love in the Western World*, rev. ed. New York: Pantheon, 1956.

RUSSELL, JEFFREY B. "Courtly Love as Religious Dissent," *Catholic Historical Review*, LI (1965–66), 31–44.

SCAGLIONE, ALDO. *Nature and Love in the Late Middle Ages*. Berkeley: University of California Press, 1963.

SCHELUDKO, DIMITRI. "Über den Frauenkult der Troubadours," *Neuphilologische Mitteilungen*, XXXV (1934), 1–40.

———. "Über die Theorien der Liebe bei den Trobadors," *Zeitschrift für romanische Philologie*, LX (1940), 191–234.

SCHLÖSSER, FELIX. *Andreas Capellanus: Seine Minnelehre und das christliche Weltbild des 12. Jahrhunderts*. 2nd ed. Bonn: H. Bouvier, 1962.

SCHMID, PETER. "Die Entwicklung der Begriffe "minne" und "liebe" im deutschen Minnesang bis Walther," *Zeitschrift für deutsche Philologie*, LXVI (1941), 137–63.

SCHOECK, R. J. "Andreas Capellanus and St. Bernard of Clairvaux: The Twelve Rules of Love and the Twelve Steps of Humility," *Modern Language Notes*, LXVI (1951), 295–300.

SCHWIETERING, JULIUS. *Mystik und höfische Dichtung im Hochmittelalter.* Tübingen: Niemeyer, 1960.

SILVERSTEIN, THEODORE. "Andreas, Plato, and the Arabs: Remarks on Some Recent Accounts of Courtly Love," *Modern Philology*, XLVII (1949–50), 117–26.

SINGER, IRVING. *The Nature of Love: Plato to Luther.* New York: Random House, 1966. (The second volume of this work is to be devoted to courtly love.)

SLAUGHTER, EUGENE E. *Virtue According to Love, in Chaucer.* New York: Bookman, 1957.

SPITZER, LEO. *L'amour lointain de Jaufré Rudel et le sens de la poésie des troubadours.* University of North Carolina Studies in the Romance Languages and Literature, 5. Chapel Hill: University of North Carolina Press, 1944.

STRAUB, THEODOR. "Die Gründung des Pariser Minnehofs von 1400," *Zeitschrift für romanische Philologie*, LXXVII (1961), 1–14.

SUSSKIND, NORMAN. "Love and Laughter in the Romans Courtois," *French Review*, XXXVII (1963–64), 651–57.

SUTHERLAND, D. R. "The Language of the Troubadours and the Problem of Origins," *French Studies*, X (1956), 199–215.

VALENCY, MAURICE. *In Praise of Love: An Introduction to the Love-Poetry of the Renaissance.* New York: Macmillian, 1958.

VINAY, GUSTAVO. "Il 'De Amore' di Andrea Cappellano nel quadro della letteratura amorosa e della rinascita del secolo XII," *Studi medievali*, XVII (1951), 203–76.

WEBER, GOTTFRIED. *Gottfrieds von Strassburg Tristan und die Krise des hochmittelalterlichen Weltbildes um 1200.* 2 vols. Stuttgart: J. B. Metzler, 1953.

WECHSSLER, EDUARD. *Das Kulturproblem des Minnesangs.* Halle, 1909.

WEIGAND, HERMANN J. *Three Chapters on Courtly Love in Arthurian France and Germany.* Univ. of North Carolina Studies in the Germanic Languages and Literatures, 17. Chapel Hill: University of North Carolina Press, 1956.

WIND, BARTINA H. "L'idéologie courtoise dans les lais de Marie de France," *Mélanges . . . Delbouille*, II, 741–48. Gembloux: J. Duculot, 1964.